THE HYPNOTIC CONNECTION

How to Influence and Persuade Anyone

Insider Secrets of a Real Hypnotist

DAN CANDELL

Author Information:
dancandell@gmail.com
www.dancandell.com

ISBN: 978-1-7326460-0-1

CONTENTS

FOREWORD

I have had the pleasure of knowing Dan Candell as both a friend and a colleague for over a decade and have always been impressed by his abilities and great work. Dan and I share similar interests in that we are both passionate about how we communicate with others and because of that we also use some of the same principals. We have both found that how we communicate with people, the methods and manner, are critical to our success in both our business and personal lives.

It also helps us, and those who interact and engage with large audiences, to establish rapport and build almost instantaneous trust. This goes a long way when you are setting up presentations where you will not only sell a concept, but also products and services at these presentations.

I also use the techniques you will discover in this book on a daily basis as a professional consulting hypnotist and success strategy life coach. The strategies and concepts in this book help me to effectively communicate with my clients in such a way that allows me to be a person of persuasive influence to them rather than just a business coach shelling out advice.

Let's face the facts here, all of us use some form of persuasion and influence whether you are in sales, hypnosis or any other service related industry, so why not just jump in and intentionally learn, study, and deliberately work more of this skill into our daily lives. This book will help you do just that. I know you will enjoy this and I wish you success in implementing what you learn into every facet of your life.

Michael C. DeSchalit
Hypnotist – Speaker – Author

ACKNOWLEDGMENTS

I would like to thank everyone and anyone who helped me with this book, and also who supported my passion and career.

Since childhood, I had a fascination with psychology and the mind. My parents and grandparents were key players in helping make sure I get the proper education and experience, and I am forever grateful.

Some personal acknowledgements:

Mom. Dad. My brother Travis. Gramps and Gram. Thank you for always being active supporters of my work and for your unconditional love.

My partner in crime. We have created so much together, and let this book be another tool that helps our lives grow.

Lisa Halpin. You are a coach, a mentor and a great friend who has pushed me to complete this book. You have helped me tremendously with writing this book and guiding me along the way.

Matt Ward. You have been like a big brother to me who pushes me and always wants the best for me. You are one of my biggest supporters. Partnering with you on our SPRH Podcast has been one of the best decisions we have made.

Michael DeSchalit. You helped me discover what was possible in putting stuff out there in the world by means of the written word. I truly appreciate your friendship and your guidance.

Jerry Valley. You are the first one who taught me the craft of hypnosis. You have kept hypnosis alive and helped me embark on a wonderful career.

Tommy Vee. You and Jerry have always believed in me and made sure I knew what I needed to know before I "hit the trenches!"

Jason Linett. Dude, you rock and I am thankful for our friendship. You continue to inspire me and make me want to be better!

Bob Martel. Since we met, you have consistently pushed me to believe in myself, and as you say… "Let the best marketer win!"

Will Horton. You got me started in the wonderful world of NLP. I have to give you credit for teaching me the true power of connecting with people through subconscious influence.

Amanda: Your sense of humor, honesty and friendship continue to inspire me. Best friends forever! One more thing, you can send me a check for including you in here.

Deb: You are the exception… enough said! You know what I mean!

There are many other people who I want to thank and also who have supported me in this endeavor to write this book. Thank you to my friends, my family, and everyone else who supported me. You know who you are!

INTRODUCTION

Do you ever wish you had a magical power that could allow you to persuade people and to get them to do what you want? Could it benefit you to know powerful hypnotic strategies that can allow you into the mind of anyone that you want? Wouldn't it also be beneficial to get into your own mind so you can achieve your full potential?

In this book, you will discover very powerful strategies that some of the world's most powerful hypnotists use to create the life they want. You will learn how to use these techniques on other people, and also on yourself to help you rise to the top in any part of your life. The great benefit here for you is these techniques seem so natural, no one will even know that you are using special mind hacking abilities to get what you want.

This book will give you the secret tools to connect with anyone in any situation. Perhaps you're in sales and need to persuade or convey a point to a prospect. Maybe you want to make more friends or develop deeper and more meaningful relationships with people. Perhaps you want to help others, or even help yourself get more of what you want. This book will provide you with the insight, tools, and wisdom to accomplish all of the above.

After talking to hundreds of people after my presentations and hypnotic demonstrations, it soon became apparent that most people didn't want to become a full-time certified hypnotist. They just wanted to learn how I got people to follow my every command. People became fascinated when I explained to them you need not do a formalized hypnotic process. All you must know are a few simple key strategies that will instantly get deep into a person's subconscious mind.

Each section of this book will cover tools and techniques you can start using right away on anyone and everyone; on family, friends, co-workers, spouses, business connections, prospects, etc. You will also learn about real-life examples of how these techniques have been used in various situations with my clients, my friends, and many others with whom I have come into contact. The result? You can quickly learn and use these strategies that will turn you into a master of getting into the mind of anyone you wish! Let's get started!

SECTION ONE
How to Hypnotically Connect with Anyone

CHAPTER 1
GETTING STARTED

My work as a Board Certified Hypnotist has taken me from coast to coast, Central America, and Europe. I enjoy the opportunity to teach people, as I've spoken to thousands of people while sharing my message. Having been known as "the hypnotist" for half my life, I came to realize that people didn't want to know about hypnotism in the conventional sense; instead, they wanted to learn how to use hypnotic techniques to form meaningful connections with people. They also wanted to learn how to better connect with their subconscious mind.

When I was a teenager, I was an outcast. My way to make friends and to be the life of the party was by performing hypnosis demonstrations. However, I soon learned that demonstrating hypnosis is not just putting someone into a trance and suggesting that they do funny things, it goes a lot deeper than that.

This book will go into depth of how to connect with people on a deep level. Within the pages of this book, you will easily learn the ins and outs of hypnotic communication and how to reach deeply into a person's subconscious mind, so you can create stronger bonds and connections with them. These styles of communication can also help you persuade and influence others to get what you want, whether it's convincing a spouse to go out for an Italian dinner instead of Chinese, influencing your children to go to bed, closing a sale, or getting a date with a love interest.

Some people may perceive these techniques as manipulation and coercion. However, these techniques are just profound communication strategies. Can they be used for manipulation? Absolutely! Within the context of this book, we will be using the techniques presented for persuasion, not manipulation.

Let's look at the difference between manipulation and persuasion (which is what hypnotic communication is all about).

Manipulation is about making somebody do something that is against their will or their interests.

Persuasion is the ability to convince someone to do something that they will find beneficial. We can accomplish this by changing the way they think, feel, and behave.

The techniques you will learn in this book are all powerful communication strategies from human psychology, social psychology, sociology, hypnosis, and Neuro-Linguistic Programming (NLP).

I teach a lot of this information to college students with confidence issues when talking with a love interest. I also teach this to salespeople who need to better communicate with their prospect or to people who need and want to persuade others in their personal and professional lives. I also instruct managers, bankers, photographers, business owners, executives, and CEOs. Can they all use this for manipulation, and get what they want? They can, and you could use this as manipulation too. However, I want to issue a word of caution. If you use these techniques to manipulate people, it will only come back to bite you in the end because people will soon realize what you are doing. However, if you are genuine in your use and ability to form deep connections with people, they will not realize the techniques you are using, because they will seem so natural.

I request you use these techniques within this book to form those genuine connections with people, and in the end, as the late Zig Ziglar said, "You can get what you want by helping others get what they want."

Get ready to open up your mind, and dive deep into the subconscious of other people so you can become a person of power, influence, and persuasion. Let's get started.

The Two Parts

This book has two parts. The first part, how to hypnotically connect with anyone, goes through hypnotic techniques that will help you open up any powerful connection with your target. We will refer to the people you are connecting with as your target.

Part two walks you through how to use self-hypnotic techniques to create your ideal personal and professional life. It talks about the right mindset to have that can help you succeed in relationships with others and also about yourself. It also teaches you how to positively program your powerful subconscious mind to get more of what you want in life, achieve your goals, gain confidence and eliminate some of the mental obstacles that hold you back from getting what you want.

The methods in this book have transformed the lives of thousands of people. I know these techniques will do the same for you when you use them effectively and often. Like any useful tool, if gone unused, it will not be effective. This book provides you with tools to help you and also influence those people around you. When you use them, you'll notice results in your ability to hypnotically connect with, influence and persuade others. You'll also be able to communicate messages to your own subconscious mind so that you can form a more positive outlook on life.

Consistency Is Key

There are two types of people in this world; those who take consistent action and those who do not. Think of two people whose lives are very similar. Let's call them Person A and Person B. They both work for the same company and hold the same position. They both are married and have two children. Regarding health, they are also pretty much the same.

They both start working for the same company in January 2015. During the job orientation, a keynote speaker talks about personal and professional growth. Person A is listening intently and thinking about how he can apply some of these principles to his life. Person B can't wait for this to be over so he can get home.

Person A has a growth mindset. He listens to podcasts and audiobooks on his way into work each day. He also works hard during his workday and gets most of his daily tasks done each day. Because of this, when he goes home, he can spend more time with his family. He also sets aside one day a week where he hires a babysitter for his children, and he schedules a date night with his wife. After working for his company for about a month, he finds an eclectic coffee shop down the road. He discovered that he could walk there and back during part of his lunch break and makes a point to do this each day.

Let's turn to Person B. He goes to work each day at least 10–15 minutes late. He stops on his way to work and gets a coffee and a donut. He listens to NPR on his way into work and on his way home he plays one of his favorite soft rock radio stations. He just wants to get the bare minimum done at work each day. Because of this, his superiors are usually sending him home with more work to do, so it cuts into his family time. He eats lunch during his lunch break, and then for the rest of the time, he walks around the office talking to his co-workers, goes on social media, and watches videos online to kill time until he must go back to work.

Let's fast forward. One month later, Person A and Person B still look similar. Two months later, there are still no real differences. Three to four months later, the changes become a little more noticeable. Person A who has now been making consistent progress has been listening to audiobooks and podcasts and gets hours of advanced knowledge and education a week, while Person B just takes in all the problems going on all over the world and gets caught up in that day-to-day drama. Due to Person A advancing his education, he is setting goals, he is taking action towards those goals, and management is noticing. Within about nine to twelve months, he starts getting promotions and accolades. He is a go-getter. He also has a happy relationship with his wife because he sets time aside for his family and his love life. Even though his life is now changing, he embraces that change and is ready for it. He also has stayed relatively the same weight and is still right where he needs to be health wise.

Let's now turn to Person B. Nine to twelve months down the road, Person B has been slacking off and management is beginning to notice. He is distracting others from doing their work, and he comes in each day talking about how much he disagrees with the new political policies being put in place by the presidential administration. He also has been putting on weight, and his wife sees how unhappy he seems because he is never really getting all of his work done when it needs to be. As a consequence, they seem to float through their marriage just as he is coasting through his job doing the minimum work required.

What's happened here? Person A takes consistent action each day to advance his learning and his personal and professional development. He has discovered ways to balance the different parts of his life, even though it can be challenging at times, he still keeps the balance. Person B takes little to no action, and he keeps doing the same things and fell into bad habits that compound and hurt his personal and professional life. However, the changes are not that noticeable until several months pass.

The point is, taking consistent action, even though that action may be small adjustments here or there will have a massive impact over the course of time. Massive inaction will yield the opposite results over time.

When learning the techniques in this book, please take consistent action. Over the course of time, you'll look back at today and see how far you've come from where you were.

Life is easier when you can make friends and have others help you along the way, isn't it? We are social creatures, and there are distinct advantages to all areas of our lives when we can win others over to our side, our cause, or our viewpoint.

This "winning personality" comes naturally to some people, while others struggle to make friends and win people over. Thankfully, it is a skill we can learn, so, it's okay if you're not born with it. Being able to make friends naturally is a learned skill. Some of us learn it a little earlier in life than others. Throughout the pages of this book, I'll show you why it is crucial to have this social skill, how you can attract people and finally how to win them over.

Being more sociable and able to bring people over to your side or your cause is one of the most important and most useful skills you can acquire. It will make your job, your personal life, and everything between easier and more fun. Here's an example.

Let's say you're on vacation and get to your hotel at the end of a long day of traveling. All you want to do is head up to your room, take a shower and rest up before starting all the fun stuff you have planned for the next week. When you get to the front desk there's a problem with your reservation and no room is ready for you and your family. With a winning personality and a good attitude, you can get the reservation clerk on your side. He or she will do whatever they can to make sure you have a place to stay and can start your vacation. In this case, this may consist of an upgrade to a suite.

That is just one example of how having a winning personality can help you in life. Of course, it doesn't end there. It will come in handy throughout your life. If you can get friendly with the neighbors, they will keep an eye out for your house while you're away. A colleague who knows you're interested in restoring cars will call you when he comes across an interesting find. Your college professor may point you toward some unclaimed scholarship funds to help you with tuition costs. Being able to attract and win the right people over can give you all sorts of big and little advantages in life.

Last but not least, life is a lot more enjoyable when you're having fun and can share it with people you like. We are social creatures, and we're programmed to work well with others. It's no surprise then that we do better and have more fun when we make an effort to make that happen. And that's what cultivating a winning personality all is about. Let's get started by taking a closer look at the importance of being likable.

The Importance of Being Likeable & Hypnotic Connections

Becoming more likable is a learned skill and something you can pick up on and work on throughout your life. Like anything new, it isn't always easy to form new habits and behavioral patterns. Being more likable isn't difficult, as you'll see in the first section, but it takes conscious effort and work. That's why I want to start by sharing a few thoughts on why it's important to make an effort and work on those skills.

When you're properly motivated to work on these life skills, you'll stick to the plan and put in the effort until those skills and behaviors have become habits. That's the end goal, to create new habits that give you that winning personality by hypnotically connecting with others. You too can become a natural at this; it just takes some conscious effort to get there.

Why Being Likeable Is Important

I alluded to a few examples of why being likable is important in the previous section, but it goes far beyond getting a room upgrade during your vacation, getting upgraded to first class, or having

suggest or call attention indirectly to

15

friendly neighbors. Being more likable gives you a distinct advantage throughout all areas of your life.

We are social creatures who live and work in a society. That means we do best and thrive when we work together. I need not tell you that it's much more comfortable and more pleasant to work with likable people. It's easier to get help with what you're doing. It's easier to manage a team and get others to do work for you when they like you.

And it doesn't stop at work or chores. Being likable makes your entire life easier and more fun. When you figure out how to be likable, how to connect with others and get that winning personality, it's easier to make friends. Being able to meet others and create instant rapport with them is a learned skill. Similar skills can make sure those friendships and relationships stay strong for years to come.

It's also much easier to date and to find "the one" when you're working on being a more likable person and form deeper, more meaningful connections with perspective mates. Much of what you do to improve your personality and make yourself more approachable and likable also works for flirting. Of course, those interpersonal skills will even come in handy as you start to nurture a serious relationship.

Being likable helps you get along with anyone at work, from your boss and co-workers to the office manager or secretary who can make your life much easier. It also helps you easily find and work with clients and customers, which can make the work you do with them more satisfying. I don't care how you earn your living. There will be situations where being more personable and likable will give you a distinct advantage over your competition and co-workers. Maybe it's something small like having your favorite office supplies available or getting your time off approved. Or perhaps it's something big like getting a promotion or getting hired because of the impression you make during the interview process.

Think about it this way. When you do your best to use the techniques in this book and develop that deep connection with people, you'll be able to reach your goals in life, no matter what they may be, more easily and faster. You'll end up with a more successful and more fulfilled life overall. It's not just getting that first promotion in your twenties. By getting that one promotion, you're setting yourself up for a much more successful career overall. That, in turn, allows you the financial freedom to invest in a better house, drive a nicer car, go on vacation, etc. And let's not forget about retirement! The more you make in your job throughout your working years, the more money you'll have in retirement, provided that you invest wisely.

Being more likable seems like such a small thing, but it can have a massive impact on your life.

Not Everyone Is Born With the "Click Factor"

Here's the deal. Some people learn to be likable and more personable at an early age. Maybe there's a genetic component to it, or perhaps they pick up these essential life skills early in life for one reason or another. In either case, it seems like they're born likable. Others are finding making friends and getting along with people a bit more of a struggle. That's ok. The good news is that having that winning personality is a learned skill. It's something you can acquire through deliberate practice which is what we'll cover throughout the rest of this book. Many people may learn these techniques only to realize that they have been using them all along but never knew these skills were inherently hypnotic.

Start Modeling People Who Are More Personable and Likable

Here's a quick tip for you before we dive into the nitty-gritty of attracting people and winning them over. You know that saying "Fake it until you make it"? Well, I am not a big fan of that. Rather than "faking it," model the behaviors and attributes of people who you view as having that likability factor. I'm serious. Think about how these "likable" people act. Think about the tone of voice they use, the body language they display, and how they behave around others. Imitate a likable person. How does that feel?

Initially, you may feel like you are just going through the motions. That's ok. Don't go overboard, but remind yourself regularly to smile, and practice your small talk skills. Keep observing people you think have a winning personality and copy little things here and there. Keep modeling that behavior and attitude, and you'll feel more comfortable with that friendly attitude. It will help you as we move through the tips and exercises in the remaining sections.

How Developing Your Hypnotic Communication Skills Will Affect Your Life Going Forward

Before we dive into the main content, let's look at how working on your likability and your personality will affect your life going forward. It will have a much more significant impact than you realize and it will influence every single part of your life from school and work to relationships, hobbies, and even where you live.

Being perceived as a likable person, and winning people over to your cause is powerful. It will give you an unfair advantage on anything, from buying a new car and applying for a new job to getting better service at your favorite restaurant. Isn't it about time you started working on these skills and making that winning personality work for you and your loved ones? Because here's the thing; getting people to like you and do stuff for you has more benefits than you may have thought. It helps your entire family and improves all of your lives. If that's not a good enough reason to get to work on this, I don't know what is.

CHAPTER 2
UNDERSTANDING HYPNOSIS & THE MIND

The clinical definition of hypnosis is the bypass of the critical factor of the conscious mind to establish automatic selective thinking in the subconscious mind. Now, you may be wondering, "What in the world does that mean?" Let me break it down to something that is "less scientific."

Hypnosis is a state of receptivity. When a person is in hypnosis, they are more open to suggestions and messages given by the hypnotist. The suggestions, within reason, are not analyzed by the conscious mind, but they are accepted by the subconscious mind. Once messages go into the subconscious mind, they become automatic and natural responses.

Hypnosis has nothing to do with mysticism or mind control. Hypnosis is a science that is recognized and accepted by the American Medical Association, neuroscientists, psychologists, doctors, therapists and even dentists.

This altered state happens naturally throughout the day. Anytime you zone out, daydream, or even go into a deep state of focused concentration; you go into a state similar to hypnosis! You also pass into a hypnotic state as you are falling asleep at night, and when awakening in the morning. The average person does not know that they are more receptive as they are waking up or falling asleep, so they usually overlook the benefits of using these naturally occurring receptive states.

What Happens in Hypnosis

When a person is hypnotized, they will remember as much as they would from any normal conversation. It just so happens, there are many conversations we are involved with that we zone out during, causing us to forget part of that conversation. The same is true with hypnosis. The hypnotic induction is the formal process that hypnotizes people. The induction distracts and relaxes the conscious mind so the subconscious mind accepts what they hypnotist is telling them without analyzing it. When a person is hypnotized, they often know what's going on around them. They can still hear other sounds and still move, but those things will not bother the person who is hypnotized.

When a person is hypnotized, often, they will feel relaxed, their limbs heavy, and their breathing natural and rhythmic. It may feel as if the person's arms and legs are so heavy they are sinking into the chair where they are sitting. For someone else, hypnosis may feel almost like lightness or buoyancy, similar to a balloon or a floating sensation. Some people are very focused on everything being said to them, whereas others will zone out and go into deep thought and "won't hear" much of what the hypnotist is saying, or for better terms, won't consciously be paying attention. However, as the conscious mind is drifting and zoning out, the subconscious mind is open and receiving the important message, even though the conscious mind may not be completely aware of it.

You don't need relaxation to be hypnotized. Think about it, when you zone out while you're driving or texting someone on a cell phone, you're not completely relaxed in a zombie-like state, right? Remember that is also a state similar to hypnosis.

The same is true for a hypnosis session. Some people feel like they are "just responding" to be polite, or may not feel as relaxed as they want, but there is no one hypnotized feeling. It's different for everyone. Some people just feel like they are sitting back listening to the hypnotist's suggestions, yet they walk out of the hypnosis office feeling and responding differently to situations problematic for them. It's normal for people to be thinking during the process, "Is this working for me? Am I really hypnotized right now? I feel like I could open my eyes at any time and walk out." A person who thinks this is correct. Hypnosis is not something that the hypnotist does to you. It's the books and movies that sometimes lead us to believe that hypnosis is mind control, where what we are doing, is a series of ritualistic processes that help the client take control over parts of their lives that they feel is out of or beyond their control. A good hypnotist will relay the reality to their client that they are not doing anything to or for them, they are working with them to achieve the desired result.

De-Mystifying Hypnosis

There are many myths and misconceptions about hypnosis, usually due to the false reality portrayed by the media, movies, and books. In this section, you will discover the common myths of hypnosis and the truth of what it is.

1) Hypnosis is sleep. This statement is false, some people may think they fall asleep during the process, but hypnosis is not sleep. Sometimes, people get confused that they are not sleeping during the process.

2) Hypnosis is mind control. Unfortunately, this isn't true. If hypnosis was mind control, let's just say I would be in a much different place. I cannot make people submit to me, nor can I use my "powers" for evil.

3) Hypnosis is a special power or is an evil satanic ritual. This one always makes me laugh. I remember when I was doing one of my comedy hypnosis shows in a small town. The local priest told his

congregation that if they went to the hypnosis show, they will be forever damned in Hell because the hypnotist would use his powers to suck out their souls and give them to Satan. A note to that Priest… the note he sent out backfired, the show sold out because everyone wanted to see what the "Evil Hypnotist" was doing. (Cue evil laughter here!)

4) You are unconscious when you get hypnotized. No. It's quite the opposite. When you get hypnotized, you are conscious the entire time.

5) You will divulge secrets in the hypnotic state. I can't tell you how often I have gotten phone calls and emails saying, "I want to find out if my spouse cheated on me and what they are doing when they go on their business trips…" Okay, if you have to ask, you probably already know the answer. That's ridiculous. If I hypnotized someone so they can tell the truth, they would actually be a better liar in hypnosis, because their responses would be more relaxed and subdued. If you must know, I don't need hypnosis to get people to reveal their secrets and deepest fantasies and desires. When a client during my intake process asks "Will I reveal all of my deepest, darkest secrets?" I lean forward and ask "secrets? Like what?" And they'll spill the beans! So no, hypnosis cannot be used to get secrets out of people; you can do that just by asking!

6) You can get stuck in hypnosis. Doctors often send me their patients for anxiety and smoking cessation, and often, the doctors will come in first before they send their patients so they can explain it better to the people they refer. I remember one doctor sat in my hypnosis chair and asked: "Dan, what are the statistics of people not coming out of hypnosis, and getting stuck?" I chuckled and said, "Well Doc, when was the last time you had someone in your clinic for a chronic case of hypnosis?" We both laughed, and he said, "point taken!" If something happened to the hypnotist while a person was hypnotized, the person in

hypnosis would be in no danger. Remember the movie *Office Space* when Peter Gibbons went to the hypnotist, and the hypnotist dropped dead and left Peter in a trance? Let's say you went to see a hypnotist, you were deeply hypnotized, the hypnotist was just about to emerge you from hypnosis, and then he or she fainted. What would happen? You would notice something was wrong, you'd open your eyes, and I hope at that point when you see the hypnotist on the floor, you'd call the paramedics. Or, you would just get bored without hearing their voice, and you'd fall asleep like you were taking a nap. Either way, you cannot get "stuck" in hypnosis.

Stage Hypnosis versus Clinical Hypnosis

Yes, it is true; I also present the comedy side of hypnosis. When I tell people this, they often ask me if I'm the type of guy who turns people into a chicken or makes them bark like a dog. I don't know where people get this idea. I have NEVER made a person cluck like a chicken or bark like a dog in my shows, nor would I stoop to that level. My shows are always fun and entertaining. I also make sure people leave my shows feeling great about volunteering, and I provide them with a very empowering message at the end of my show. As a result, I get a lot of private clients from my shows and demonstrations. Often, when someone comes into my office, if they have seen my show or been hypnotized by me in a show, they ask, "How is this different?"

Stage hypnosis is real, and when done correctly, it displays hypnotism as an excellent example as a modality for personal and professional change and transformation. But the primary purpose of a stage hypnosis show is to entertain and highlight the creative talents of the people who volunteer for the show. People attend these shows with that expectation. A person hypnotized on stage is entirely aware of what they are doing, but hypnosis is a tool to lower inhibitions on stage, producing almost an intoxicating effect, and the hypnotist's suggestions become the volunteer's reality. On stage, the hypnotist will have people hallucinate an alternate reality, such as becoming movie stars, orchestra conductors, dancers, singers, etc.

Clinical hypnosis (sometimes called hypnotherapy) and stage hypnosis are two entirely different animals. If I told one of my office clients to stand up during our session and dance like Miley Cyrus, would they? No. Why not? That message would not be congruent with what they want to achieve. Hypnotherapy helps a person change their thoughts, feelings, habits, and behaviors, NOT to entertain themselves or the hypnotist.

With clinical hypnosis, we can help people change habits such as smoking and nail-biting, eliminate procrastination and increase motivation, lose weight by changing cravings and eating habits, control stress and anxiety, and even control pain and heal faster after surgeries. I use hypnosis as a tool to help people overcome challenges, to break free from anxiety, to gain confidence, and to re-program their minds to get more of what they want in life and achieve their full potential. I am an expert at high performance. I specialize in helping people overcome anxiety and also help salespeople, business professionals and athletes reach higher levels of success. Those are the areas I specialize in, and I use hypnosis as a tool to help those issues. Every hypnotist is different. Some hypnotists are specialists and will specialize in a few areas. Others are generalists and work on every subject under the sun. I am a fan of finding a specialist who can help you with your goals.

Self-Hypnosis

Self-hypnosis was my first introduction to hypnotism as a personal change modality. I learned self-hypnosis when I was a teenager to help with focus, concentration, and memory retention. The one question I would always get asked would be, "How can you wake yourself up?" Since you're not sleeping while hypnotized, you can't "wake up," but you can emerge yourself. It's as simple as opening your eyes.

You can accomplish a lot of the same thing with self-hypnosis as you could with going to a professional hypnotist; however, if you have more complex issues you need to resolve, I highly recommend seeking the help of a professional hypnotist. Working with a Certified Consulting Hypnotist can lead to faster and sometimes more effective changes and results.

Self-hypnosis is a zone you create yourself. When you create this receptive zone state, you can suggest to yourself how you want to be or be different. There are many ways to do self-hypnosis. You can learn self-hypnosis from a good book on the subject, from taking a class, from audios and even from recording your hypnotic process into a recording device and playing it back.

Understanding NLP

When developing a hypnotic connection with someone, it is also necessary to have a general understanding of Neuro-Linguistic Programming. NLP is a way of influencing the cognitive behavior of a group or individual by using language patterns and subconscious communication skills. Think of NLP as hypnosis without hypnosis, a conversational or waking hypnosis.

Richard Bandler and John Grinder co-founded NLP in the 1970s. They studied human behavior and quick and effective ways to get people to change their internal patterns. They looked at the human mind like a programmable computer. The theory (which has been shown to be correct) is that if you can re-program and update a computer, we can look at the mind and human behavior in the same way. We can upgrade a person's belief systems and behaviors in the same way we update a computer's operating system to work more efficiently. Imagine trying to run a computer program from today on a Windows 95 operating system. It just wouldn't be possible.

However, that's how many people are living their lives, with outdated programs and perspectives.

We all have our own map of the world, and NLP helps us connect with and work within our target's map of their reality. When we understand their reality, we can change it by re-framing their perception of reality. However, before we change their programming, we first must meet them at their level.

I use a lot of NLP in everything I do. I use it as a natural way of communicating with people, and I also use it in my hypnosis practice to help people change on a faster and more efficient level. NLP is all about effective communication to "crack the code" if you will go to a target's concept of reality, or what they consider a reality.

NLP is also used to help with deeply rooted problems holding people back. It is used to cure fears, phobias, and lifelong anxieties. It has also helped people with severe clinical depression, schizophrenia, and other mental issues. NLP is also famous for helping people change habits and behaviors and also for helping athletes and others who need more of a winning mental attitude such as people in business and sales.

This is all good news. It means if Olympic athletes, multi-millionaires, and even presidents have benefited from NLP, surely you can too, and help connect with others on a profound level.

Bypassing the Critical Factor

How to communicate to the subconscious mind is through a process called "bypassing the critical factor of the conscious mind." The critical factor is like a filter that keeps information from getting to the subconscious mind unless it belongs there. Five basic principles bypass the critical factor. When this filter is bypassed (or lowered), it can form new habits or programs, evoke emotional states, or influence a belief or the way we perceive something. I often hear people express concerns that their "guard will be lowered," and are often afraid that the result can be catastrophic; however, our critical factor is bypassed naturally every day through many sources. Let's get into the most common ways to bypass this mechanism, or "lower the guard," so that you can be aware of them, and how to use these principles in your communication.

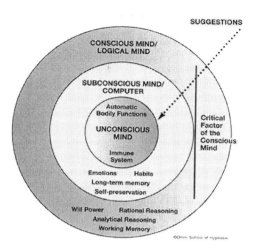

These five ways to bypass the critical factor are:

Heightened Emotional States

Anytime you experience a heightened emotional state, your guard is lowered, and information naturally enters the subconscious mind. This is often how fears and anxieties form. Fear is a heightened emotional state where a person can experience a fight or flight response. Negative emotions will usually result in a negative mismatched program that forms. For example, someone may be anxious when they walk into a sales presentation even though they know there is no reason for them to be afraid. This could stem from when that person was a child and got criticized in a classroom, and that mental program could have been generalized to all presentations or situations where they must talk in front of people.

In the same way that negative emotions bypass the critical factor of the conscious mind to form new programs, positive emotions will have a similar effect. When people experience positive emotions though, they will often feel good about the decisions they are making, and the people around them. Therefore, it is crucial that in your communication strategies, to build the "know, like and trust factor," you evoke positive emotions in your target. Imagine if you are selling your services or product to them, and they are feeling happy and excited about it, they will feel much better about listening to you, and

關鍵因素　　27

> Anything repeated several times no longer becomes analyzed. It becomes a natural outcome.

the resistance goes down. When you evoke positive emotions, you can also get people to make decisions faster and easier, feel better about the decision they are making, and have their choice benefit both you and them.

Here is one of the biggest compliments I receive after I do my presentations, keynotes, and seminars, "Wow, Dan, we had so much fun in your presentation that we didn't even realize how much we actually learned until we left the room." When people are having fun, and positive and powerful emotions are elicited, their barriers are lessened, and they are more open to learning and taking away essential points. That's why you may have heard that it is useful to start a presentation off with a joke. It gets people laughing, so they are taking away key points they don't even realize they are taking away until it is rooted in their mind.

Repetition Is the Mother of All Learning

You may have heard this before: "repetition is the mother of all learning." This statement is true. Every time something is repeated, it knocks on the critical factor until it lowers that guard and gets into your subconscious mind. That is why advertisers say it takes 7 to 11 repetitions of a message for a target or prospect to take action or decide about the product. Think about things you just do naturally, habits or behaviors you have that you don't even have to think about anymore. Brushing your teeth, tying your shoes, opening a door, driving a car. You don't have to sit there every time you open a door and analyze how to do it, do you? Of course, not! You have repeated that action/behavior so often that it becomes a natural part of your powerful subconscious mind. That is why you should use repetition of a message when communicating with your target. Often, people will misinterpret this principle and think they must repeat the same sentence or phrase repeatedly, but you don't have to use the same sentence or phrase over again, you can use repetition of a concept or idea conveyed in different ways.

Think of jingles or product slogans you hear on the radio or television. As soon as a commercial plays, they have a jingle associated with a particular product so when you hear the jingle, you think of the product. That is due to having listened to that jingle several times. That is also why in commercials and advertisements you will often hear phone numbers, websites, or services repeated at least three times. It creates a link in your memory with the information they want you to record and remember.

Authority and Credibility

There are just some people that we build such a high level of respect or trust in that everything they say is held in high regard. That is often true with religious figures. When people enter a church, synagogue, temple, or any other religious institution, our critical factor becomes bypassed. The same thing is valid with parents, coaches, doctors, and some political figures. Without getting controversial here, if you want to see a great example of mass hypnosis, the next time you walk into a church, and everyone stands and sings at the same time, ask yourself "Am I hypnotized?" Authority figures set our expectations, condition our beliefs, and will often influence our behaviors.

How do you use this principle in your communication with your target? It's quite simple! Use certificates, social proof, testimonials, and newspaper clippings to position yourself as the obvious expert in your industry. Imagine walking into a doctor's office, and seeing a wall lined with degrees and certificates, you immediately establish more trust in that doctor because their degrees and certificates are usually an indication of their credentials. That is also why referrals work. Think about it. Someone who you trust is giving you a referral, and that creates an expectation that the professional you will hire will do a good job. It's the same if your friends set you up with someone to go on a date. They may say, "Oh you'll love this person!" That sets up an expectation based on the credibility of your friends.

Age Is a Factor for Belief and Learning

Remember how when we were children, we just believed what we were told? We believed in Santa Claus, the Tooth Fairy, and maybe even the Monster living in the closet! It's not that younger children do not have a critical factor, but it's still being formed, therefore, it is very easily bypassed. It's hard to say specifically at what age our critical factors become stronger, as it's unique to every individual. However, children are always in a state of learning, so what is presented to them is usually not analyzed on a deep level.

Think of the programs we have acquired in childhood. Some are good and some are bad. Many people carry around childhood traumas for the rest of their lives and wonder why they have a hard time letting go of those traumas. Now you know; it's due to the bypass of the critical factor and those programs become a natural part of who we are and how we respond.

You might be wondering, "Great, but my targets aren't children!" That's ok, but we can still create that childlike learning state in adults. Here's how. Assuming someone had a positive childhood, you can evoke a childlike emotion that could easily evoke a positive childlike experience and relate it to your product, service or request. One example is this, "most of my clients report that when they use our product or service (inserts your product or service here), they feel like a kid on Christmas again… Remember when you were little and that excitement you got from opening a gift on a birthday or holiday? Well, that's how most people describe our services, it's like they are just as excited as they were when they opened a gift on their 10th birthday!" By doing this, you are creating a childlike emotion and feeling state, and you are transferring that positive emotion to you, your product, or service.

Conventional Hypnosis versus Hypnotic Communication

I've been known as the hypnotist since I was about 13 years old. I would zap people into a hypnotic trance in the middle of the lunchroom and classes, and I would even hypnotize some of my teachers. I want to be clear about this; these people were willing participants. I also performed stage shows and still do, I hypnotize large groups of people on stage in front of a big audience and have them perform entertaining acts. I also do traditional hypnotherapy to help people overcome anxieties, self-doubt, confidence issues, and also help athletes and salespeople when at the mental game of sports and selling. So, what is the difference between conventional hypnosis and hypnotic communication?

With conventional hypnotism, you're putting somebody into a trance-like state. They are a willing participant, and we use that trancelike state to change a behavior, feeling, emotion or habit. We evoke this trancelike state by applying a hypnotic induction. The hypnotic induction bypasses the conscious mind and allows the hypnotic suggestions to be accepted as if they were real.

Hypnotic communication does not require a hypnotic induction. It also does not require a person to be willing nor does the person have to be aware that they are being "hypnotized." It can still have very similar effects to putting somebody through an actual hypnotic process.

That brings up the ethical and moral obligations and issues again. However, please know that it is very complicated and near impossible to get a person to do something that they would not be willing to do. However, think of a family member for whom you would do anything or another person with whom you have a meaningful connection. What lengths would you go to for that person? These connections and techniques can have a very similar effect.

Some people might think, "I can't be hypnotized." But this is a state we go into every day several times a day. Anytime you daydream or zone out; you go into a more receptive state. And that's all hypnotism is. It's a type of zone, a responsive state that bypasses the conscious mind. So, any information that is given to the person is not analyzed, it just goes naturally and directly into their subconscious mind. Think of a person engrossed in their cell phone, maybe on Facebook or texting. They are so consumed in that world, that they become oblivious to the outside world. While their mind is focused on their cell phone, Facebook, or text message, that is their conscious mind that is preoccupied with activity while their subconscious mind is open. While a person's subconscious mind is open, they become very receptive and suggestible. That is an excellent time to put something into their mind without them critically analyzing it. Therefore, this naturally evoking trance state will cause a person to be very receptive to outside suggestions. That can produce a very similar effect to going through a hypnotic process with a formalized hypnotic induction that causes a person to go into a receptive trance. Using the waking hypnotic techniques I will be sharing with you throughout this book can also produce a similar effect as evoking a formalized hypnotic trance.

The Conscious and the Subconscious Mind

You must understand the difference between conscious communication and subconscious communication. The conscious part of the mind is a very analytical, logical, critical part of the mind where information is analyzed. However, to change a person's habits, patterns, beliefs, feelings, sensations, emotions, etc., we want to get into the subconscious part of the mind. We do this by bypassing the conscious, analytical, critical mind. The way that you'll be learning how to do this is with hypnotic communication will allow you to connect with anyone hypnotically so what you say will bypass the critical mind and get directly into the powerful and natural subconscious mind.

Think about a person you spend time with, and every time you're around them, they have this natural ability to lift your spirits and put you in a great mood. On the opposite end of that, there are people you associate with that we called a fun sponge. They seem to suck all the fun, happiness, and joy out of even the best of situations. Wouldn't it be great to be the person who can positively impact a person's state of mind, mood, and emotional state? Using this form of hypnotic communication, you'll be able to do precisely that.

Conscious versus Subconscious Communication

The conscious mind is the very logical and analytical part of the mind. The last thing you want is for your target to be analyzing every word that comes out of your mouth. The more people overanalyze what you are saying, the more they have a chance to build doubt, fear, resistance, and objections against you. The subconscious is the part of the mind that stores all of your experiences and also composes your thoughts, feelings, emotions, behaviors, feelings, and habits. We want to communicate with that part of the mind so we can bypass any analytical thinking, knock down any resistance, and build trust with our target. When you communicate directly to the subconscious mind, the target is more likely to accept what you say as the truth because you are evoking emotions, feelings, and sensations that can influence their behaviors, habits, and decisions. That can be used in any sales situation or relationship.

Upon first learning how to connect with someone hypnotically, sometimes people think they will use their voice or their words to zap a person into a trance. However, there is much more than just hypnotic language, although you will learn a lot of hypnotic language in this book. The words we speak only forms 7% of the way we communicate. The other 93% comprises nonverbal communication. Much of this is in body language. You can tell a lot about a person by their posture, their gestures, the way they move their hands, and even their eye movement.

CHAPTER 3
CRACKING THE COMMUNICATION CODE

Connecting Through Values, Ethics, Morals and Perspective

Everyone has a personal set of values, ethics, and morals. Some of these are learned whereas others are developed through experiences, and others are innate. Values are the backbone of who we are and what we do. Our values can explain why we click with specific people and situations and why other situations repel us. Once you know your values, you'll be able to understand your core purpose. When you know what others' values are, you can connect with and communicate with their values in mind.

Our values, ethics, and morals and even core purpose can also help explain why we attract specific people and even why we are happy in some situations and miserable in others. If you are unhappy with your job, living situation or relationship, it's usually because your values or at least one of them is not met. Often, when I am working with someone who expresses being unhappy in some part(s) of their life, about 90 percent of the time, it's because at least one of their values is not being met, or every situation they put themselves into is going against their values.

Let's look at an example of someone who is extremely anxious and depressed about their job or work situation. Perhaps, some of their values are freedom, variety, and flexibility, but the job they have is very structured and repetitive. It drives them crazy because they aren't allowed to express themselves like they want to.

Let's take a look at relationships. Perhaps to one spouse, creativity and seeing things many ways is very important. To the other spouse, they are very analytical and only see things in black and white. They loathe creative types. Some people would think this would be an apparent mismatch, but sometimes, you are not aware of these differences until much later into a relationship, and that is when they become problematic.

Do you have to have the same values as a spouse or partner? Not necessarily. Your spouse should at least support your values, and you, in turn, should support their values. When you are supportive and understanding of each other's values, you can support each other for who you are, and what is essential to each of you, even if you don't see things the same way.

The same thing goes for situations. If you like nature and openness, then living in a tiny studio apartment in the middle of the city probably isn't conducive to happiness and fulfillment. If freedom and flexibility are important to you, then having a structured job probably isn't the best option for you.

You may be wondering; how does this help me connect with people? It's simple. Knowing and understanding others' perspectives and values can give you insight into how to play into those values. What does this mean for you? It means that to connect with people, your values can be defined, but your viewpoint should be one of openness and flexibility. The more open and flexible you are, the more supportive of others values you can be.

What's Behind Your Eyes?

They say that the eyes are the gateway to the soul. You really can tell a lot about a person by the way they move their eyes. I'm sure you've heard that you can tell if a person is lying or telling the truth just by looking into their eyes. You can tell how a person is thinking and even what they're thinking by observing their eye pattern movement. We call that eye-accessing cues. We will get more in-depth into this a little later on in this section.

The Hypnotic Gaze

When you think of somebody being hypnotized, you might think of a hypnotist uncomfortably and awkwardly staring into a person's eyes. I often make a joke in my hypnosis shows that a hypnotist without a voice is just a creepy man (or woman) staring at you. I'm sure you've also heard the famous words from the hypnotist, "look into my eyes." That is not as ridiculous as it sounds, and there's a reason we do this. There is something that we call "the hypnotic gaze." Hypnotists use this as a form of establishing power and authority over their subject or target. The hypnotic gaze is when a hypnotist will authoritatively stare at their target. But they're not necessarily looking into their targets' eyes. It's almost as if they're looking through the person between their eyes on a focal point that's slightly behind the target. If you ever see someone with glasses lower them down to the base of their nose and stare over the glasses in an intimidating way, it has a very similar effect. However, this is something that hypnotists use in a hypnotic setting such as in a hypnotherapy office or stage show. When hypnotically connecting with your target, you don't want to intimidate them. You want to do the opposite. You want to make your target feel comfortable.

You might be wondering; how much eye contact you should be making with your target. In American culture, sociologists tell us that 70% eye contact is appropriate when communicating with another person. If you're using less eye contact than that, the other person will think you're not paying attention to them and are disengaged. If you use more eye contact than that, your target will think you are trying to dominate them. So, when you're talking to another person, maintain eye contact with them for about 70% of the conversation. You might be wondering when I'm not looking at them, what should I be looking at, or what should I be doing? When you're not maintaining direct eye contact with them, you can maintain indirect eye contact or look slightly to the left, slightly to the right, slightly up or slightly down. Think of when you go in deep thought while another person is talking, you're thinking about something they just said. Are you still awkwardly staring at them? Most likely not, usually you are looking in one direction or another with your eyes slightly up to the left or slightly up to the right and you probably are forming an image in your mind of what they just said. If a person thinks that you're not paying attention, you can say something like, "I am paying attention, I'm just trying to get the image in my mind."

Others might wonder, "Do I look directly into their eyes?" You do not have to look directly into a person's eyes; if it's difficult to do, you can pick a spot between their eyes, or focus on the tip of their ear. They will not know the difference.

Cracking Your Target's Communication Code – Eye Accessing Cues

Here is where it gets interesting. As I mentioned, you can tell how and sometimes what a person is thinking by their eye pattern movement. Everyone is a little different and everyone might respond to things differently. However, these studies and eye accessing cues are formed by how the majority of people respond.

Think about this for a moment. You're trying to think of a word that is on the tip of your tongue, but while you're trying to think of this word, you're not looking a person the eyes. Your eyes shift in a certain way that helps you gain access to the missing information.

When you're telling a fictional story, and you're trying to create the next thing that's going to come in the story, your eyes shift in a different direction. So, what does all this mean? What does this tell us?

When a person's eyes shift up, and to their right, they are usually forming a mental picture or image in their mind. When a person shifts their eyes up and to their left, this usually means that they're trying to remember or recall a particular mental image or picture in their mind. Note: when you're looking at someone, their right is your left and vice-versa.

Visual Creation versus Visual Recall

Knowing this information, if a person is telling you a story and their eyes are shifting up and to their right, they're trying to create that story. If someone is trying to remember something, their eyes go up and to their left. So, if you're asking a person about how their day has been going, and their eyes shift up, and to their right, they are usually trying to make something up off the top of their head. That does not mean they are lying; it could mean they are creating the story of how their day went. However, if they shift their eyes up and to their left, you know they're actually trying to remember how their day went so they can give you an accurate description.

Auditory Responses

The same thing can be said for sounds. When a person's eyes shift up and to their right, this usually indicates that they are trying to create a sound or conversation in their mind. When their eyes shift to their left, this usually means a person is trying to recall or remember a sound or conversation they heard.

Internal Self-Talk Cues

When you see a person shift their eyes down and to their left, this usually means that the person has an internal dialogue that's running through their mind. If you see a person's eyes shift down to the left and then their right, what some would call being "shifty-eyed," they usually have an internal struggle.

Accessing Emotions

When you're conversing with someone, and they look straight down while shifting their eyes to the right, this usually means they are accessing emotions and could mean they are uncomfortable.

What Do You Do with This Information?

Now that you know all this, what do you do with this information? This information can help give you insight into what and how a person is thinking. Study their eye pattern movement and their body language. You'll be able to tell better how a person communicates. When you see a person looking to the left, or to the right as if they are looking at their ears, you know that they are more auditory communicators. When a person is looking up and to the left or right, you know that they are more visual communicators. Generally, when a person is looking down, you can tell they communicate more through feelings or emotions. Knowing this information about a person can help you better communicate with them, because now you'll know if you should direct their focus on their feelings or their emotions, or on sights or sounds.

You can also gain insight into how a person communicates based on what they use. If they say things more like, "I hear you loud and clear," then you know they are more auditory communicators. When a person says something like "I know how you feel," or even uses temperature or other feelings to describe something, like, "that seems to be a hot topic," or "that puts a pit in my stomach," then you know that they learn best through their feelings emotions and sensations. On the same token, when a person uses words such as, "I see your point," or "I see your side of the story too," you know that they are more visual communicators.

Once you discover how a person codes information, as visual, auditory, or emotionally, you can communicate that preferred method. These are slightly more advanced strategies, but once you understand them and start observing people, they will be beneficial for you to know.

Additional Notes and Techniques to Use with the Above Information

With the initial contact made and hopefully a little bit of rapport established, it's time to talk about winning people over. This section consists of tips and strategies you can employ to make people more comfortable around you. They will make you more approachable, more likable, and more charming. Choose what applies to your core personality and your particular situation. Not all of them will apply to every situation, but sooner or later, they will all serve you well. Let's dive in.

Start by Listening and Observing

When you're trying to win people over and be your most charming self, the first inclination is often to hijack the conversation and talk as much as possible. You feel like you must work hard to present yourself at your best. Stop! That isn't the best approach.

A much better and more effective approach is to sit back and focus on listening and observing first. While you may have met the other person or group of people, you don't know them yet, and even if you do, you don't know what's on their mind right now. Take this time to pay attention to them. Listen to what they are saying. Observe their body language. Pay attention and gather as much information as possible. It will come in very handy going forward.

Make It About Them

Once you have been observing and listening for a bit, it's time to show interest and become a more active participant in the conversation. Use the knowledge you've gained by making it all about "them."

Think back when someone you've met has shown interest in what you do or what you have to say. It feels good, doesn't it? Provided the interest is (or at least feels) genuine, it leaves a very favorable impression. People like it when someone else is interested in them, and in turn, they like the person. Use this to your advantage by always making it about the people with whom you're talking.

That works even when your goal is to win people over to your side or get them to do something for you. It's all about perspective and coming up with a win-win scenario. Think about how the other person can benefit from helping you out and then focus on that aspect of it and make it about them, instead of about yourself. Focus on how helping you now will benefit them and how you will both benefit in the future. We will go more in depth on this topic in the next chapter.

Adapting Your Communication Style to Meet Theirs

Now you know how to listen, observe, and find out how your target is communicating. Once you pick out their communication strategies and styles, you can match theirs, and communicate on their level. Once you do, this will open a deep connection with the person or people with whom you are creating that connection.

CHAPTER 4
BUILDING THE KNOW, LIKE AND TRUST FACTOR

Rapport and Your Mindset about Rapport

Hypnotic communication and influence are all about the ability to get people to accept your suggestions and to take action on them. Before doing this, you must get them to a level where they trust you, feel safe with you and are secure in the decisions they are making with you. The foundation is what we call the KLT factor, or the "know, like and trust factor."

In my hypnosis practice, it is my job to change people's lives quickly. I get a lot of referrals from therapists and doctors, and they only give me about 4 to 6 sessions to help people eliminate mental and emotional baggage, so they can become healthier mentally, physically, psychologically, and emotionally. However, when a therapist refers someone, that therapist usually has gained that person's trust over several months or even years. I'm sure you've heard of people who have gone to a therapist or a psychologist for years and years, and they're still stuck in their path of turmoil and mental and emotional baggage.

When a client sits down in front of me, I must use techniques that build rapport and a deep connection with that particular person within 5 to 10 minutes that would usually take somebody 5 to 6 months to develop. Before I teach you the techniques on how to do this, develop what we call the "know, like and trust factor," we first must get into your mindset so you understand what and how to think about the people with whom you want to form this connection.

The NLP definition of rapport is getting people to feel understood by you. That is a great definition which gets straight to the point. Here's how I want you to look at this… Someone with whom you are in rapport is someone with whom you have a connection. You both can carry on a conversation for hours, and maybe it feels like you've known that person forever. Perhaps you have known them forever.

Right now, I want you to imagine somebody with whom you'd like to click naturally. Think of a person with whom you'd like to form a connection. This person can be a spouse, a family member, a love interest or a friend. Imagine conversing with this person, and it just flows naturally. You feel like you have a deep connection with them and you want the best for them, and they want the best for you and from you. We will call this person, Person A.

Now think of somebody who you don't click with. This person rubs you the wrong way. There's just something about them that you don't like. You feel turned off by them, and you would never listen to them or take advice from them. We will call this person, Person B.

Now imagine that you are going on vacation, and you have $5,000 in cash you need someone to look after. The banks are closed, your house is undergoing a renovation, and you need someone to look after this $5,000 in cash until you get back. Who would you trust? Who would you willingly give that to? Would you leave it with person A or person B? I bet you would rather give your money to a person you trust and feel a deep connection to.

Now, let's take it a step further. You are in the market for buying a brand-new car. Now, this is not just any car. It's your dream car. You sit down with someone, and they remind you of someone very familiar, but you're not sure who it is. You feel this deep, meaningful connection with the person, and they are genuinely passionate and interested in helping you out. However, just because you're cautious and you want to make sure you're getting the best deal, you go to a dealership down the street with the same car. The car might be a couple of hundred dollars cheaper, but this person seems like they are entirely uninterested in what you're asking for and what you want. They aren't listening to you; all they are interested in is the final sale. To take it a few steps further, they are talking trash about the dealership you were just at a couple of hours ago. They fulfill the description of a slimy used car salesperson. Who would you feel more comfortable purchasing the car from? I bet you would want to do business with the person you had that deep connection with, right?

That is what I want your mindset to be about, rapport. When we form a deep connection with somebody for whatever reason, if you wish to date them, sell them something, or become friends with them, I want you to remember this. I want you to view this transaction like two friends working together to create a common goal. And when you think of one of your close friends you click with naturally, the conversation flows, in fact, you could finish each other's sentences; you would be right to assume that you have an excellent rapport with that person as they also have a great rapport with you.

Whenever I sit across from a person in my office, I must view our roles in each other's lives as two friends helping each other to get to a common goal. The common goal we both have is for them to get better. When I have this mindset about them, I can begin to see them how they need to be and also see them at their best. When you do the same with people you approach, and you view them with this mindset, you will notice that the chemistry naturally flows between you two.

Rapport is the foundation of all persuasion, influence, and connecting with people hypnotically. Once you are in rapport with the person and they are in rapport with you, you can begin influencing them and persuading them to do anything.

How to Build Rapport Quickly and Effectively

Now that you have the right mindset about rapport let's talk about how to build rapport, and also why it works so well, you will find rapport is the foundation for building a hypnotic connection with people.

The fact that makes this all come together is that people with people like themselves. Think back to that good friend you naturally click with, if they were the complete opposite of you, you probably would not click with them. But what is it that makes us feel that connection with people? It's something that we call mirror neurons. Have you ever seen someone and said to yourself, wow that person is so stylish? And then you remember that you have the same outfit you just wore the other day? Or have you ever noticed that when you're talking to a friend, you're talking at the same rate of speech, pitch, tonality, and even volume? Maybe you're both whispering, and you're close together, so you make sure you never miss a word that the other person says.

The fastest, easiest, and most efficient way to build rapport is to fire off those mirror neurons. So, how do we do that? It's quite simple. It requires that you become a little observant and flexible so you can meet people where they are. That is utilizing a technique we call matching and mirroring. Many people do this naturally, but they're not aware of it. Recognizing this and knowing when to use it can be of great value and can give you a strong persuasive advantage over others who do not know these techniques.

Matching, Mirroring and Modeling

Some people think that matching and mirroring means copying or mimicking their target. We don't want to mimic them or copy them; we want to model them subtly. Doing this will cause those mirror neurons to fire off, and it will cause the other person to feel they connect with you because you understand them and you are like them.

Some things we can match and mirror are postures, gestures, movements, and positioning. If you're sitting across from someone, you can sit in a similar way they are sitting. You don't have to sit exactly the way they are, but you should sit similarly. If they gesture with their right hand, you can make a similar gesture after waiting for a few beats or later in the conversation. People make a mistake by thinking they must keep up with the other person and constantly copy their gestures. Many people think that if their target moves their left hand, then they should move their left hand in the same exact way at the same exact time. However, that's going to get you caught, and it will turn people off instead of firing those mirror neurons.

So here are some things that you can match and mirror or model in a person. Earlier I mentioned matching physical posture and gestures. You can also match and mirror speech. You can become aware of their tonality, the rate of speed at which they talk and the volume at which they speak.

A person came to my office last week, and this person naturally talks loudly. Even though the doors were closed, I was convinced that the people in the office building down the street could hear this guy. So, I needed to quiet him down, but I had to do it in a nonabrasive, polite, and natural way. It's important to note that once you are in rapport with the person, you can begin leading them and influencing them. You are going to their level; now it's time to bring them to yours.

So how did I get this guy to quiet down? I started talking loudly like he was. I started using common gestures and words he was using. He was sitting with his left leg crossed over his right, so I sat with my right leg crossed over my left. After a few minutes, I knew that we were in rapport because we just clicked. If I moved and changed my body posture, he would move and change his body posture. If I leaned forward, he would lean forward; if I leaned back, he would lean back. Now he was subconsciously following me, and I became the leader. So gradually, I lowered my voice down and spoke in a slower and more relaxed tone. I sat back in my chair and asked him questions in a soft tone. Within just a couple of minutes, he too was speaking in a soft tone and was very relaxed. He made a mental, emotional, physical, and psychological shift in merely five minutes. That is the power of rapport.

I remember I was sitting in an airport, and there was a row of four people sitting across from me. I wanted to see how far I could push this skill and see how deep I could go. I started with the person sitting to the far left across from me, and I matched his posture and gestures. I then did the ultimate test, I yawned, and sure enough, he yawned also. I knew I had the click factor with him. So, I moved to the woman sitting to the right of him. I matched her gestures and her posture. All the while, the guy to the left of her was also matching me and as a result, was matching the other woman sitting next to him and sitting across from me. Within about 10 minutes I had the whole row of all four people in sync with what I was doing. It was like some big brainwashing experiment. I lifted my left hand, and they all lifted their left hand, I scratched my forehead, they all scratch their forehead. I was having a lot of fun with this until someone sitting next to me caught on to what I was doing. I was in Georgia at the time on my way home from speaking to a large company of sales representatives and teaching them these techniques, and the woman sitting next to me stood up and screamed at me and asked what I was doing to those people. That pretty much broke the connection I had established.

Why Does This Work?

Words only make up 7% of our communication. That means the other 93% is all nonverbal communication. That encompasses everything from posture, to eye pattern movement, to breathing, to eye blinking, to the facial expressions we make. When we fire off those mirror neurons and model and match people, we are sending their subconscious mind signals that they can trust us and they can be safe with us. That's why sometimes people will feel so comfortable with you they may divulge their deepest darkest secrets. Yes, with great power comes great responsibility.

The Hypnotic Handshake

If you have ever seen one of my shows, demonstrations, or presentations, you may have noticed me shaking people's hands and putting them into hypnosis instantly. That works by interrupting a person's usual pattern, disrupting their equilibrium, and firing the commands directly to their subconscious mind that causes their nervous system to briefly shut down by producing a state of simultaneous confusion and relaxation. I will often go up to a person during the show or demonstration to shake their hand, and as I am shaking their hand, I will shake it with an abrupt motion and say the word "SLEEP!" This interrupts their mind for a brief moment, and it bypasses their critical mind and fires the command right into the subconscious mind causing them to close their eyes and go into a relaxed state as if they were sleeping. Now, when you're trying to connect with the person hypnotically, I don't suggest this is how you do it. Here's why.

At the time I am writing this book, Donald Trump has now been in office as president for a little over a year. And when the hypnotist community saw how Donald Trump was shaking the hands of world leaders, they had a field day with this. The hypnosis forums online were lighting up with hypnotists calling out Donald Trump for doing the "hypnotic handshake" on the world leaders with whom he came in contact. If you watch videos of him doing this, you see him shaking their hands, forcefully pulling them forward, and he whispers something into their ear. We know as hypnotists this is a way to bypass a person's conscious analytical mind and get directly into their subconscious mind. We can all only imagine what he was whispering in people's ears as he did this. Shaking hands in this manner is also a way to establish dominance over a person. When you are hypnotically connecting with people, they don't want you to feel dominant over them; they want to feel an equal connection with you.

Here's how a handshake can help you hypnotically connect with the person and help them feel an equal honest connection with you.

First and foremost, even though I think this way of a handshake is natural, and I think it comes naturally to other people, when I started teaching sales seminars, I realized it wasn't. I often find myself teaching people how to hypnotically and properly shake hands for about 45 minutes. Then, I developed a one-hour workshop on how to hypnotically shake someone's hand to connect with them, and it sold like hotcakes. Several organizations and teams of sales professionals would hire me to teach this workshop to their sales team. It might sound funny, but it was advantageous for people to learn.

There's a lot of debate about how to shake a person's hand. I'm sure you've heard everything from shaking a person's hand with a death grip to lightly shaking a person's hand like a dead fish. In the next section, you will learn about matching, mirroring, and modeling. That's precisely what we're going to do with the handshake. When you shake someone's hand, you should match their handshake. If their handshake is firm, yours should be firm. If their grip is light, yours should also be light. That signals the subconscious mind saying, this person is like me. One other subtlety that many people miss is what you do with your facial expression when you're shaking a person's hand. Imagine you saw someone in a restaurant you have not seen in a long time, and you like this person. You would most likely be very excited to see them, and you might raise your eyebrows in surprise. Whenever your eyebrows rise, it's a signal to other people you are excited. That's how you want the person to feel whose hand you're shaking. You want to send the sign to their mind that you are excited to see them and meet them, and that you are very similar to them. However, you don't have to say that to people. They will think you are weird if you say that to them. Instead, state that in your body language by matching their handshake and raising your eyebrows as if they are a friend you haven't seen for a long time. That will send that subconscious signal that will help build rapport.

There's one more thing that I like to call the hand over hand. Some people think that when you're shaking hands with another person, that you should put your free hand over theirs. That is only socially acceptable as you are leaving the person, not when meeting or greeting the person. So, just be aware of this. Again, practice this as much as possible until it becomes natural. The idea behind this communication is that it becomes a natural thing for you to do.

Focusing Attention on Them

Your ability to focus your attention towards others helps you to gain a hypnotic connection. That is why it is so important to learn how to listen, ask appropriate questions, and show a sincere interest in what they do and want.

Remember, this is all about an equal and genuine connection. People don't like to hear continually, "I, I, I" or, "me, me, me." There should be a balance that shows you are interested in what they have to say, and when you show a genuine interest, they will often reciprocate and be genuinely interested in what you have to say. It can be a little difficult to develop this habit, but with practice, you'll become very aware of its power. The best way to develop this habit and technique is to become aware of how you are responding to people, and avoid saying things like, "Me too," or, "Yeah, I know," or "Good for you." Show genuine interest and ask questions that relate back to what they're talking about. That will send off a connection in their mind that you genuinely care about what they're saying, you're interested in what they're saying, and it will start building that connection. Here's a sample conversation:

Them: "Hey, I just went on vacation!"

You: (Instead of saying, "Yeah, I went last week!") "Really, where did you go?"

Them: "I went to New Hampshire."

You: "Really, what did you like about New Hampshire?"

Them: "There was this store there that was cool, it was called Zeb's!"

You: "No way! Is that the store that has all of those various foods and sauces?"

Them: "Yes, and they have candy and a bunch of other fun stuff. Why, have you been?"

You: "Yes, I've been. I got a bunch of stuff there and brought it home. What did you get?"

See, in this conversation, you're putting in genuine interest, and you are relating the conversation back to them in the questions you ask, but it also opens up a connection with the things in common.

I would often hear one of my close friends talking to people at social events, networking events, and even with their spouse, and this person would always try and "one-up" what everyone else was saying. The problem was that they had no idea they were doing it, and they were belittling others that they would talk to, and it turns people off. If the person they were talking to said something like, "my kids are sick," they would respond in a way to try to one-up them and say something like, "Really? I've been sick for the past three weeks." First off, I have found that people don't care that much about what happened to you, at first. That's why they are telling you first what is happening with them, and when you show interest in them, then they will care more about what you have to say.

Have you ever been in a conversation where you know nothing about what the other person is talking about, nor do you care? People get bored quickly if the discussion is not something they know a lot about, or are interested in. However, what gets a person to feel good and enthusiastic is when somebody listens to them about their interests. Think about this for a moment, don't you get excited when somebody talks to you about one of your interest or hobbies you have? Those are the people you want to spend more time with, right? So, what happens if someone talks about golf, and you don't like to golf? Do you pretend also be interested in the game? Absolutely not! Never fake interest or pretend you have something in common. People will find out quickly that you're not genuine. Instead, just play the role of an active listener. Ask well-informed questions. People like to be the expert, so if you're asking them questions and they sit in the seat of being the expert, it will bring their energy level up, and you'll see their energy shift to being excited and enthusiastic. To shift somebody's energy, just get them talking about something that they enjoy doing.

You Have Rapport. Now What?

Congratulations! You have established a subconscious connection with your target. Now, this is where the real fun begins. Once you have rapport, you can start a process we call pacing and leading. Think of it as you are taking the controls now. Establishing rapport is all about meeting people on their levels of communication. Sometimes we have to lower down to meet them where they are, and sometimes we have to rise to meet them where they are. Once those mirror neurons are fired, and we established the connection that caused the target to think, "Hey, this person is like me, and I like them because they are similar to me," we can now get them to follow us. Remember the example I used about the loud guy in my office we had to quiet down so the people in China wouldn't hear him? The same thing goes for people at the airport. Once you gain rapport, they follow you. Think of it as having a conversation while running a race. You and your target both start off at the same pace, and you are having a conversation while you run. Then you speed up slightly, and to keep the conversation going, the target must speed up too. Then you start slowing down, and to stay in the conversation, the target must slow down also. You are leading them to stay at your pace, but you started off running at their pace first.

When building rapport, practice it until it becomes natural and a subconscious way of communicating. You want that feeling of being in sync to be natural. To do this, you must practice with your friends, your family, strangers, and anyone and everyone you meet. However, a word of caution follows. When people feel a deep connection with you, often they will open up to you, and they will tell you things you probably don't want to or need to hear.

I remember performing a hypnosis show in New Hampshire for a high school. Before the show started, the principal of the school came up to talk. For me, matching, mirroring, and modeling have become natural and innate. However, I was using these techniques on the school principal and didn't even realize it. Within a matter of about three minutes, he said, "Hey, you know, you are easy to talk to, I feel like I could tell you anything..." He started talking about all of his financial problems, his marital problems, all of his doubts and insecurities and went on about some of his sexual difficulties. In the midst of him disclosing this information to me, I heard my cue to go on stage and start the show, so, I put out my hand and said, "Sorry, stop right there, they're introducing me to run on stage, that's my cue to start, we can talk about this after." I just made sure that after the show I packed up my stuff quick and ran out before he had a chance to finish pouring out all of his difficulties.

Once you establish rapport, you can make small adjustments to your communication styles, and the target will most likely follow you and model your communication styles. Think about ways you can use this for beneficial purposes. If you're talking to a person and they seem sad or depressed, and you want to elevate their mood, you go down to their level of communication and then work your way up to a more lighthearted way of speaking and feeling. At that point, they will follow and model your mood, your communication styles, and your positive attitude and emotions.

Sometimes people will follow your mood subconsciously. I was recently working with a teacher, and she was coming in for anxiety and positive thinking. She initially said, "I need to learn ways to deal with my students. Every Monday, they are awful, so every Sunday night; I stay up worrying about how horrible my kids are going to be, and how much strength I am going to need to control my classroom!" After talking for a while, she realized that it's not just her kids in her classroom. It's her and her expectations! She goes in every Monday morning ready for battle, and her students can read that body language. They expect that from her. So, we worked on her changing her expectations, and sure enough, her students matched her mood, good or bad! Sometimes we think we shut off negative emotions, but we don't, and then it negatively affects others. We can influence people without even realizing it!

What Not to Do When Building Rapport

Remember, when matching, mirroring, and modeling, we are not copying them. Some people think that they must be a carbon copy of their target. That cannot be further from the truth. For example, if you have short hair and your target has long hair and curls their hair around their index finger, don't attempt to mimic that! You'll be twirling air!

As we touched on before, these connections with people must be genuine. One of my good friends is a chameleon in all social situations. He can adapt to any situation but does it so it compromises his integrity. He agrees with people's opinions no matter what they say, just to form that connection with them. Someone will say to him, "I love to watch baseball, do you?" And he will say, "I love to watch baseball too!" Ten minutes later, someone else will talk about how boring watching baseball is, and again, he will agree with that person and say, "I know it's such a waste of time!" The irony in this whole thing is that he gets caught ALL THE TIME! People will overhear him giving conflicting information and call him on it all the time.

The message here is to find commonalities that will bring you together. There is no need to fake interests to match theirs, and there is no need to compromise your morals, ethics, or values to try and fit in. We do not have to mesh with everyone. Never be afraid to cut off a connection or break rapport if you think there should not be a connection to be made.

What If I Get Caught Using These Techniques?

When I teach these techniques to executives, managers, and sales professionals, the one common question I always get is, "Dan, what happens if I get caught? What do I do?"

Let me first say this; if you use these techniques with good intent, and you are natural about them, you will not get caught. I have been using these techniques for over ten years and have not only used them on thousands of people, but I have also taught them to tens of thousands of people, I have only been caught once.

Let me explain. I often work with sales professionals on boosting confidence and building an unstoppable mindset so they rise to the top of their industry. I was working with a client on these issues, and within the first ten minutes of the first session, we were clicking well! But then something strange happened, we both started matching and mirroring each other, and he stopped me and said, "Um, Dan? Am I matching you, or are you matching me?" He worked for a big web-based sales company, and one of the courses they offer there is an introduction to rapport. Guess who taught that course? Yup! Yours truly! He knew what to look for, and he knew I did this, and went in with the mindset, "I am going to be super aware of what he's doing." So, yes, he caught me. We just laughed it off, and I said, "Well, now you know I practice what I preach, and now I know you were paying attention!"

So, knowing you will most likely never get caught (unless you are deliberately copying or mimicking your target), people still have the question, "What do I do?" If someone catches you, you can take two tactics. Option number one is to play it off as if you have no idea what they are talking about, you thought you two just had natural chemistry (which if you use these techniques, it should be natural so you won't be lying to them.) The other option is to own it and say, "I just naturally model and mirror good traits that I see in people. I guess it's just my natural way of communicating."

CHAPTER 5

CLICK!
THE COMPLIANCE FACTOR

Getting a Person to Do What You Want Them to Do

Sometimes it can be as easy as telling your target exactly what to do. I know it's hard to believe but hear me out on this one. We're so used to being told what not to do, how not to feel, how not to behave, how not to react. There are significant problems with this. The subconscious mind, where all of our feelings and behaviors and habits are stored, does not understand negative outcome words. So, whenever you tell a six-year-old, "Don't touch that hotplate," what did they do? They touch the hotplate even though you told them not to. When you tell an anxious person not to be nervous, what happens? They will feel more nervous. Even if you tell a person, "Don't forget to take out the trash." They will forget to take out the trash. But why does that happen, and what can we do about it?

Being a person of influence means getting people to act and behave by how they want to behave. When you get people to feel how they want to feel and do things they want to do, you will be their hero, which will open up a greater and deeper connection with them.

It takes a little bit of work but focus on reframing every negative command into a more favorable and positive outcome. Instead of telling people what you don't want them to do, tell them what you want them to do, what they ought to be able to do, or what they should do.

Instead of saying, "Don't be nervous," you can frame it more positively and say something like "just let yourself go into it feeling relaxed." Instead of telling a person, "Just don't think about it so much," or, "stop worrying," you can frame it in a different and more positive oriented way. "Move your mind to something else; think more positively, better thoughts produce better results."

It is a proven fact that we get more of what we think about. If people are always thinking about the negative outcome, or if they're always focusing on how not to feel or what not to do, they get more of that. They feel more of that unwanted feeling, they do more of that unwanted behavior; they end up giving into that habit even more even though they've been trying to stop. By helping people focus on what they can do or how they want to respond, react, behave, or even think, you'll help people feel more at ease and put them into more of a solution state of mind.

Words to Avoid

Just as there are words you want to use, there are also words you want to avoid. You want to avoid words that convey doubt or uncertainty to your target. These are words such as:

- Can't
- Try
- Could have
- If

- Should
- Might
- But
- Would have

More Positive Outcome Examples

People of influence and respect use positive outcome language and commands. They focus on the desired outcome of what they want others to do instead of not do. As you become aware of this, your life will change. Here are some examples:

Instead of telling people, "don't be late," it will be more effective to say, "be on time."

Instead of saying "don't sign on that line" it becomes "sign on this line."

It is also true with your inner self-talk. The reason this works (using positive outcome language) with yourself and your targets, again boils down to how the subconscious communicates. The subconscious mind does not hear negative words. When you tell someone "don't be nervous," the subconscious mind hears "… be nervous." The more you focus on what you want people to do, respond and react, the more positive influence and effect you will have on people and yourself.

Your Positive Mental Attitude

Never underestimate the power of a positive attitude. Part of forming an excellent hypnotic connection with someone is to elevate their mood. We can do this by boosting our own attitude. I'm sure you've heard the saying, "Misery loves company…" We all know people like this. When they are miserable, they ruin everyone else's day around them too! Here are two good hypnotic ways to elevate a person's mood and mental attitude to get them to feel better around you and about you.

The Elevation Method

I like to call this the elevation method because it lifts people's mood and creates this "instant click" feeling with the other person. It will sound straightforward and basic, but it's very effective. Remember, this must come from a genuine place. Here is the formula.

Complimenting Question + Smile + Head Nod = The Click Factor

Never underestimate the value of a smile, a compliment, and a head nod. I remember I was at a conference about to give the opening keynote about how to get and stay motivated. I was a little nervous because no one knew who I was, so I knew I had to start rubbing shoulders with the higher-ups at the conference. Then I spotted a woman who was on the company website, in all the videos on the website, and who everyone was doting over. She was clearly a VIP. I knew if I got in good with her, then I would be all set, and she would introduce me to more important people. Her name was Sarah.

When doing prep work for the company, I saw Sarah in a lot of videos and photos promoting the company, and one thing she did well was she conveyed a fantastic level of passion and enthusiasm. She radiated positivity and empowerment. So, I went up to her when she seemed free for a minute, and I used the Elevation Method.

I said, "Hi Sarah, I'm Dan. I'm giving the keynote address today, and I just wanted to say how great it is to meet you in person finally." She said "In person? Have we met another way before?" I replied, "Well when doing some research for my presentation, I watched a lot of videos and saw you in them. How is it that you always make everyone feel so good about themselves in a sixty-second video?" I smiled and gave a slight nod as I said this.

What this did was it let her know that she was important, it gave her a specific example, and it warranted her to provide a reply to the question other than just saying "Thank you!" She replied, "Well, a lot of work goes into those videos, but honestly, I just imagine on the other side of the camera is my close friend that I am having a conversation with." That was four years ago to the date I am writing this book. That opened up a great connection with her, and she still, to this day, boasts about how good I made her feel, and she gets excited every time we see each other or talk. And of course, I mirror that same level of excitement because I feel the same way.

Remember, before you go up to a person, pick out something (genuine) that you can complement them on, and form that into a question. For example: "Janet, that's such a great scarf, where did you get it?" When you say the compliment part of that question, smile and give a very slight nod. This bypasses the analytical mind, and it puts them in a more positive emotional state, and it opens them up to find the response to your question. It takes them off guard in a good way and elevates their mood.

A smile goes a long way. I can't tell you how often I have smiled at someone in a coffee shop and said, "thank you" for holding a door open for me, and they reply with, "you have no idea how great it is to see someone smile!"

Remember also, the head nod. When I am presenting to a group, and I want to form a more agreeable state with the people in the group, I always nod my head like a bobblehead doll, and you will be amazed. Soon, everyone will start nodding their heads back at you.

Nodding your head can form a more agreeable state with people. It is a subconscious signal that says, "This is right," or, "It's okay to agree to this," or, "This works." However, don't go overboard. I have seen some people with a huge grin on their face and vigorously nodding their head and looking at their target creepily in the eyes... don't do this. Remember, this should all be natural and smooth flowing.

CHAPTER 6
PERSUASIVE HYPNOTIC LANGUAGE

Hypnotic Persuasive Language

Now we get to the part that people often associate with forming hypnotic connections with hypnotic language. As I said previously, the words we use only compose 7% of the way we communicate. So, let's make those words as powerful and impactful as possible. You'll also learn that it's not just what you say, but how you say it.

Hypnotic persuasive language bypasses the critical and analytical part of the mind so what you say is not analyzed. Let's look at some words and phrases that can have a dramatic impact on your target's ability to trust you, believe you and accept what you say as accurate. The hypnotic words I will teach you are called truisms. Some words have social and emotional proof to them, so they become challenging for people to deny. When you use these words in sentences and your communication with people, often, what you say after these words, the target must accept as truth. You can

> By using hypnotic language, you can influence their outcome and their buying decision.

use these words in sales, with a spouse or partner, and even with complete strangers to allow you to cut in front of them in a long line.

Most people: This hypnotic phrase "most people" is a powerful one. Whatever comes after the phrase, "most people" is not analyzed by the conscious mind, and it goes right into the subconscious mind. This phrase works because it plays on our psychological needs and insecurities. If we disagreed with "most people," then it plays on our insecurities of being left out. As humans, we don't like to be left out, but if we are left out of what most people do, say or think, then we can have feelings of isolation and loneliness. Therefore, it is easier to agree to what follows this statement. Let's look at some examples of how this technique can be used.

"Most people who tell me what you just told me will choose this option here."

"Most people in your situation would use this."

"Most people who know what you know will make a decision now."

This technique is used best when you want to get people to decide on something or make a specific choice. You can help them narrow down their selection and then lead them to choose the best option for them. Using this strategy will get them to think they made that choice all on their own, and that option they picked is the best one.

A variation of most people is to say something like, "If you are like me, and like most people, then…"

Everyone knows/everyone says: This one works based on the same concept as most people. The psychological thought process here is "if everyone knows this, then I must know this too because I am a part of everyone!" This technique works well with commonly known phrases and truisms (see below) that are difficult to deny.

"Everyone knows the early bird catches the worm…"

The Three Powerful Words That Build a Deep Connection

Just as building rapport through matching, mirroring, and modeling is important; using these three magic words is also amazingly effective.

Feel, Felt, Found: This one is one of my favorite ways to build rapport and also to overcome objections and eliminate doubt in people. It sounds like this "I know how you feel, I have felt the same way before (or, I know someone who has felt that way), and I have found (or, they have found), that when _____.

That gets your target into a more agreeable state and makes them feel understood by you. Here is another example. "I know how you feel, that it seems too expensive; many people I have worked with have felt the same way when they first hear the fee, but then when they experienced results right away, they found that they were happy that they made a decision right away and that it was actually very inexpensive for what they were getting."

I was working with a soccer player for more confidence, and once she brought confidence into her game, she reported that she wanted to connect better with people on her team. She was from another school, and the other girls on the team knew each other, so she felt like an outsider. She reported that the girls were talking about one of their friends, and she wasn't sure how to be a part of the conversation if she didn't know the girl they were discussing. After working with her on strategizing what she could have said using this technique, we came up with something like this.

"That's really funny! I know how you feel, I have a friend who is just like this girl that you're talking about, and when she kept acting like a 'mean girl,' some of her good friends wouldn't talk to her anymore. Is that what happened to your friend?" Notice how we didn't have to use the three words exactly, (feel, felt, found), but it has the same effect.

Using this technique can help you relate to people on a deeper level and help them feel like you understand them. Once you have this connection, you can recommend solutions, and they will be more open to listening to you.

Embedded Hypnotic Commands

Embedded hypnotic commands are hidden commanding phrases that prompt your target to take action without having the target realizing you are telling them to do something. In my hypnosis sessions, we use these all the time to help a person achieve a deep level of hypnotic receptivity (trance). We do this by hiding suggestions that the target feels little to no pressure to comply with, so they just will automatically do it. An example can be something like this "As you're sitting here and we are having this conversation about wanting to go into hypnosis now… you may find that the things I say are very easy to achieve." The embedded command is "go into hypnosis now." This command is not analyzed by the conscious mind because it's hidden amongst other words.

These embedded commands don't just have to be in the spoken language; they can be in text format, as well. People often ask if it's possible to be hypnotized by reading something. Yes, you can. It happens all the time. We often "trance out" when reading, and we put ourselves in the world that the author is trying to convey to us.

A few weeks ago, I texted my friend and wanted her to call me. The text read "You can call me if you want to hear what happened." There are two embedded commands here. One is, "you can call me" and the other is, "you want to hear what happened."

Here are some other examples of really crafty embedded suggestions. Again, please remember that these may seem obvious, but I promise you, they sound so natural when you use them, that they are not heard by the conscious mind. They are heard and given meaning by the subconscious mind.

What if you could get people to feel they like you from the very beginning? Here is a way to do this using embedded hypnotic command.

"You, like me, _____."

We are telling the target they like us without telling them they like us. It sounds like this, "You (pause), like me (pause), understand the true value of these techniques." Again, the subconscious applies one meaning to what you are saying while the conscious mind hears something that has a different meaning. However, the subconscious meaning will always win over. Remember, the subconscious is the automatic and natural part of the mind; and what gets in there sticks.

Here are two great ways to make this technique even more powerful. As you are saying, "You, like me..." gesture in towards yourself, bringing the attention towards you, and at the same time, slightly nod your head yes. That will send even more subtle non-verbal cues to the subconscious mind. Powerful? You bet!

By now (buy now)

This one I learned from a dear friend. The same principles are applied where the conscious mind hears one thing, but the subconscious mind hears another and applies that information to your automatic responses. That is great to use when selling something and you want to condition them to be ready to buy. When you say something like, "By now, we have reviewed all of the options, and you must be ready to make a decision." Or something like, "Now you know all of the features, so by now, I'm sure you must be ready to make a decision." What we mean by saying these statements is a time reference "by now." However, what the subconscious mind hears is "BUY now!" Interesting, isn't it?

Recognizing These Techniques

Many people do not realize how much and how often they are being persuaded to act, behave, or react in a certain way. Advertisers, marketers, politicians and even religious figures and institutions are continually using powers of persuasion to try and get us to act in a certain way or even believe what they want us to believe. To become aware of these techniques, watch commercials and look at advertisements and look for embedded commands and hypnotic language such as the words we were going over previously. By doing this, you can easily become aware of how you may be persuaded without even realizing it. Once you recognize these techniques and how they are used, you can resist against them, or at least be more aware if you are acting on your own free will, or if your decisions, beliefs, and behaviors are being influenced.

"You could either _____, or _____?"
"Would you rather _____, or _____?"

These are great leading phrases when presenting options or choices. It's what we call an assumptive question. That assumes that they will choose one of the two options you are offering. That works well when setting appointments with people "you could either come in on Tuesday at 9:00 am or Thursday at 2:00 pm." It also works great when choosing between two price points. "You could either choose the $3,700 program or the $5,300 program." Again, you are assuming that they are choosing one of the two.

You can use this one for a spouse as well. "Honey, would you rather have Italian or Chinese food tonight?" Just be careful, when your spouse catches on, they may say, "Neither, I want Mexican!"

That is also an effective technique to use on your children when you want them to go to bed. "Jake, do you want to go to bed now, or in ten minutes?" You are making them think they have the freedom of choice. Little do they know, it's all in your hands.

"I wonder..."

You may notice that some of the language we have been using is vague and some are open-ended. A lot of hypnotic communication is letting people come to their own conclusions. Even though you are leading them, they will still think that their thoughts, ideas, and "choices" are free will. Little do they know, you are leading them exactly where you want them to go. The words "I wonder" will cause your target to think about what you are saying and see your side of things.

"I wonder if you'll see my point of view."

"I wonder what if you'll be able to see the bright side of this."

"I wonder if you'll end up dumping your boyfriend and go out with me instead." (I had to sneak that one in there.)

CHAPTER 7

USING EMOTION TO CREATE HYPNOTIC CONNECTION

Heightened emotional states are really useful when influencing, persuading, and connecting with people. Imagine what it would be like to strike up any emotion you want in a person. Think about the potential you would have to influence them. You, like me, see the power in doing this, don't you? (See what I did there!)

You can easily convey a positive or negative emotion in your target and connect that emotion to any place or anything you want. I know some business owners who use this unethically. They will evoke a very negative emotion in their customer or prospect and connect that negative emotion to their competition. The same goes for love interests. I have seen people manipulate a love interest to feel a very negative emotion and connect that emotion to their current partner, and then evoke a positive emotion and get their love interest to connect that to them. You can only imagine the moral and ethical problems with this. But remember, if people are manipulated into doing something they do not want to do, it will come back to bite the manipulator in the butt.

Manipulating or coercing a person to do something they do not want to do or buy something they do not want to buy differs from persuading. Persuading is helping influence a person's behavior or decision, to make that decision easier. Often, people will buy something on a whim or because they feel a certain emotion even though they do not need or want what they bought. Later, when they get home, they will often realize or at least stop and think, "Wait, I really didn't want nor need that. Why did I buy that, I am going to return this!" What results is buyer's remorse, and the victim will often regret their decision, feel taken advantage of, and resent the person they felt took advantage.

Remember, emotions are one way that bypasses the critical mind. When a person experiences a heightened state of emotion, their subconscious mind is more open and receptive, and whatever happens around or connected to that emotional state/time will often create a behavior or a response in the target's subconscious mind. You can do this by evoking a positive emotion or a negative emotion and connect or relate those emotions to something to get your target to think, feel or respond in a way you want them to. One of the positive ways to lower barriers is by using laughter. When people are laughing and having fun, they rarely have their guard up, it's lowered down, and they are easier to influence because they are not expecting to be sold or swayed or even learn. One of the highest compliments is when a person takes one of my classes and says something like, "Dan, we were laughing and having so much fun that we didn't even realize we were actually learning!"

There are several hypnotic emotion evoking words that will cause a person to go to a time where they felt a certain way or create a time where they would feel that way. These emotions we evoke in people are called "arousal emotions." It's not like it sounds. These are emotions that keep your target alert and interested in wherever you direct their attention. These emotions should be substantial enough to get a reaction out of people, and the emotional buzz words will help with that.

The first step, before you evoke emotion with one of the emotional buzzwords is to identify how you want them to feel, or how they should feel. What do you want them to feel? What should they feel? Why should they feel that way? Now let's get into the emotional hypnotic buzzwords that can help evoke these emotions.

Emotional Hypnotic Buzzwords

Imagine, picture, visualize, think about, think about a time when...

These are words and phrases that evoke emotions and feelings in the subconscious mind. Remember, when you evoke emotion, you are getting to the subconscious mind which will allow your target to see themselves feeling good about deciding.

You can use any combination of these words, in fact, mix it up a little! You will want to mix it up because everyone communicates a bit differently. Some people will report they can think about something, but they have a hard time imagining it. Others will say they can picture something, but not visualize, and all other combinations.

Let's look at a few examples of how this can work.

Let's first work with evoking positive emotions. Let's pick an example of asking someone to go on a date. "Think about how much fun we will have when we go to the baseball game; it will be just like the time we saw each other at Jamie's party and laughed so hard we were spitting out our drinks! Remember that? I don't even remember what we were talking about, do you? So, when should I pick you up so we can go to the game?"

You want to move them through the emotional ladder to get them in a more positive state. When we feel better about something, we will be more likely to agree and say yes!

That can also be helpful in a sales situation. Let's say you are trying to sell someone a computer. Before you use any of the emotional buzzwords, you first want to find out their motivation for buying the computer. Let's say they need a computer that is faster and has more memory. They are sick and tired of waiting 5 minutes to open a program, and they hate having to carry around an external hard drive. Knowing this, you may say, "Imagine taking the computer home and being able to use it right out of the box. Say goodbye to all of those old issues. Think about how much faster you'll be getting things done on your new laptop, and you can look forward to keeping everything contained so that you can leave that old external hard drive behind!"

Anchoring Positive Emotions

You may have already caught onto this, but you can anchor a positive emotion, or a negative emotion just as easy as it is to evoke that emotion.

Once you evoke that emotion, you then have the target picture themselves feeling that emotion about you, your product, or service. In the baseball game example, we had the target go back into their memory and think of a time where they felt good. After accessing that feeling, it was then connected to the baseball game — so, they saw themselves feeling the same good way in the future situation.

You can do this with negative emotions as well. Evoke them and attach them to something. Without getting too political, you see this happening with a lot of political figures. When you look at a commercial around election time, it starts off with evoking a negative emotion by showing some horrible images, such as little children starving, people dying in a hospital bed, or some other very gut-wrenching image. Then it says something like, "This is what will happen if you elect (insert candidate here)."

Maya Angelou said, "People may forget what you say, but they will never forget how you made them feel!"

So, go out and strike some emotions in people. Make them feel good, and they will remember you for it.

The Strength of Exciting Emotions and Love

I see many people in my hypnosis practice for confidence issues. For some, this involves confidence for dating. Once we increase the feelings of confidence, reduce the feelings of anxiety, and establish an unstoppable state of mind, people often ask me "What is the ideal first date?"

A lot of studies have been done on what to do and where to go. Believe it or not, studies have shown that going to the movies is the worst first date you could go on. A good first date should start off with something that elevates levels of excitement and something that gets endorphins flowing. When we start that flow of endorphins, we feel good, and the level of oxytocin and dopamine (the chemicals responsible for love and happiness) also flow, and we connect those feelings to the person. If you are going to incorporate a dinner into the date, it's best to do the invigorating part of the date first, and then go to dinner afterward, because then you can talk about those positive experiences.

CHAPTER 8
BUILDING COMPLIANCE

Hypnosis is all about building a more compliant and agreeable state. It is very difficult to hypnotize a person who is not compliant or agreeable generally. However, once in this state of compliance, you can influence the behaviors, decisions, and feelings of another person. The words, phrases, and techniques I will share in this section are all great ways to connect, persuade and influence others hypnotically. However, before you start building compliance, rapport and trust must be developed to get the best results. Once you have that know, like and trust factor, these techniques will be powerful.

The words and phrases in this section bypass the critical mind and influence the subconscious mind. Like many techniques we have gone through, a person will not likely analyze what you are saying when presented with these words, phrases, and techniques. Practice them every chance you get so you get used to using them, so they become more natural, and so they become your automatic way of communicating and connecting with people.

The Power of "Because"

What if you could get a compliance factor of 94 percent? That means 94 percent of people you talk to agree with you, give you what you want, and will feel good about giving you what you want? That would be amazing, right? Well, here is one technique that can do exactly that!

Remember when you were a child, and your mom or dad said, "Don't touch anything in the store!" You may have asked "why?" and they retorted back, "Because I said so!" There was nothing open for discussion after that. Using the word "because" can help bypass the critical mind and help you get more of what you want and persuade others to give you what you want.

In 1978, Harvard Professor Ellen Langer conducted a study to test compliance with the word "because." Professor Langer had students try to cut in front of people in line while using a popular copy machine on campus and measured the compliance levels based on the excuses given. The researchers had participants test three responses. The results were astounding.

"Excuse me; I have five pages. May I use the copy machine?"

"Excuse me; I have five pages. May I use the copy machine because I have to make copies?"

"Excuse me; I have five pages. May I use the copy machine because I'm in a rush?"

Did the wording affect whether people let them break in line? Here are the results:

"Excuse me; I have five pages. May I use the copy machine?" [60% compliance]

"Excuse me; I have five pages. May I use the copy machine because I have to make copies?" [93% compliance]

"Excuse me; I have five pages. May I use the copy machine because I'm in a rush?" [94% compliance]

Using the word "because" and giving a reason resulted in significantly more compliance. That was true even when the reason was not very compelling ("because I have to make copies").

The researchers concluded that people went into an automatic agreeable state and that hearing the word "because" will cause a higher level of automatic compliance.

www.psychologytoday.com/blog/brain-wise/201310/the-power-the-word-because-get-people-do-stuff

When you want people to comply, act or behave in a certain way, use the word "because" and add a reason after. You'll get that agreeable factor much easier!

Ask a Set of Questions That Warrant a Positive Response

The following is a technique that can stack the odds in your favor of building a more compliant and agreeable state. It would be great to get people to comply with you automatically, wouldn't it? You can see how you can use these techniques, can't you? You'll be pleased as you make deeper connections with people, won't you?

The more we agree, the more agreeable we become, right? Okay, I know, I have been using this technique all along. This technique is called "The yes set." It is a very popular technique used by powerful and effective sales professionals.

You use this technique by asking three questions you know the response will always be a "yes." The great thing is these questions don't even have to be connected or related to the topic you're discussing. "It's a beautiful day today, isn't it? I hope we have more days like this, don't you? So, let's get started, shall we?"

You are getting people used to saying yes, and this forms a more agreeable state, so they will be more likely to feel good about saying "yes" to your other requests.

A note about these questions: you can make them even more effective by have them end in "wouldn't you, don't you, can't you, etc." type of questions. They will be more natural than just asking a question that requires a person to think too analytically. Asking, "The sky is so blue today, isn't it?" will have a much more effective response than asking, "Isn't the sky blue today?" Starting the question with an undeniable truth statement and ending it with a question will take the thought processes out of the response. When building agreeable states, you don't want people to stop and analyze what their responses will be. You want everything to flow and become subconscious. When people are analyzing what you are saying and how they will respond, they are using the conscious part of their mind. You always want to make sure the communication is all subconscious.

The Law of Reciprocity

As we continue with our theme of compliance, there is a widely known concept called the law of reciprocity. It is a principle that states when somebody receives something, they feel more obligated to give something back in return.

I remember when I was in high school, I read a book called, *The Art of Schmoozing*. It was all about the law of reciprocity and primarily how to schmooze your way into and out of any situation. It talked about how getting little trinkets at the dollar store and giving them out to people can go a long way in getting what you want. Let's just say it takes bribery to a whole new level.

Using this principle, I remember being a junior in high school. There were about 1,400 kids in our school, and we had four administrators. We had a principal and three vice principals. Around Christmastime, I used to make candy cane reindeer for all of my friends and give them out to people. It was something I spent a whole weekend putting together, and I would make about 40 or 50 with pipe cleaners, pom-poms, and those little googly eyes. Then I came up with an idea. Some people in school were giving me a little bit of a hard time, and if those people positioned it correctly, it could look like I was the one at fault. I looked at these candy cane reindeer, and I thought to myself, "What a great opportunity to win over the administration!" Some people might have considered that brown nosing; I felt it was a gift to them and a gift to myself. So, I wrote each administrator a little card and wrote something sweet and innocent on the card. I put the cards and envelopes in their mailboxes and taped a candy cane reindeer to each card. The next day, one by one, each administrator called me down to their office to thank me. All of my teachers must've thought I was getting into trouble as they saw me get called to the principal's office, and then each vice principal's office. Then I figured, why to stop there? Why not hit up the nurses and the school secretaries as well? By the end of the week, the entire staff of the school knew who I was, and I soon became one of their favorite students.

It worked in my favor. I was never a troublemaker, but I was a little bit of a funny, goofy student. I wouldn't go as far as to say I was a class clown, but I would like to have fun with my teachers. However, some teachers didn't get my sense of humor. Even when I tried to get in trouble, just to test the boundaries, the administration would tell my teachers what a nice guy I was and to give me some slack.

This principle can apply to many different aspects of your life. Think about being in a relationship, nowhere out of the blue you by your spouse a dozen roses and have them sent to their office. You can only imagine what you'll get in return. I remember talking to a married couple I was working with in my office. The wife said to the husband, "If you do the dishes, I'll give you a back rub..." The husband replied, "What will I get if I do the laundry and take out the trash?" Let your imagination run wild with how the wife responded!

The law of reciprocity is evident in all areas of life. Think about a time when you went out to dinner, and the server brought you over your bill. Studies have shown that people will increase a tip amount by as much as 30% if the server gives the bill, starts walking away, and then walks back and takes a couple of pieces of candy out of their pocket and puts them on the table. When we get something, it causes a psychological need to want to give something back.

We see this principle used a lot in business. In my business, I give away a very simple solution to a person's problem in exchange for their name and their email address. We call this a lead magnet in the marketing world. There's a space on my website where people can put in their name and their email address and get a free video training of some sorts. This builds credibility, authority, and rapport with the person watching the video. Usually, at the end of the video, there is an option for them to sign up for something that they have to buy. The thing that they have an option to pay for is usually a small investment under $20. Then, when people pay the more modest investment, they'll be more likely to spend a larger amount of money with you later on.

The adage, the more you give, the more you get back in return, is sometimes applied here, but just like all the other principles, your intentions with this must not only benefit you, it must also benefit the other person. Think of areas where you can use the law of reciprocity in your life. You can use it personally, professionally, in your relationship, and with your family. Some people may consider this a bribe, but it's playing on a deep psychological need that we all have. That deep psychological need is one that prevents us from wanting to feel feelings of guilt from owing somebody something. Owing somebody can cause feelings of guilt and shame, so when someone gives us something, we feel like we should give something in return.

Note:

Go to
www.HypnoticConnectionBook.com
to be enrolled in the **FREE** companion course that goes
with this book

SECTION TWO

How to Hypnotically Connect
with Yourself

CHAPTER 9

HYPNOTIC CONNECTION WITH YOURSELF

How to Hypnotically Connect with Yourself

Congratulations! You just learned how to connect with others hypnotically. But this book would be incomplete if there wasn't a section on how to communicate better with yourself. This section of the book will teach you the right mindset to have about your new ways of communicating. It will also show you how to develop a more successful mindset for connecting with others and taking action in your own life.

This section will help you tap into your own mental power and potential. Your mind is like a computer with psychological software that allows you to organize your thoughts, your feelings, your actions, behaviors, and habits. If there is a behavior or habit you want to change, it's just a matter of conditioning or programming your mind to upgrade that software.

After working with thousands of people to have a more successful and high achieving mindset, I have found that most of the people's problems stem from programs running on out of date software in their subconscious mind. Using the techniques in this section, you will learn how to update your mental programming just like we would update a smartphone or a computer. Imagine running an old out of date program suited for Windows 95 on a modern computer system. It just wouldn't work optimally. That's how many people are floating through life, trying to run old out of date mental programs on a different software system in their mind; it's just not going to work. As adults, we still let programs run our life. The consequence can be spending unnecessary time and energy worrying we are not good enough and being our own worst critics. However, the good news is, this can be changed a lot easier and quicker than most people think. We will do this by reprogramming some of your thoughts, feelings, and behaviors.

There are three things internally which control us our thoughts, our feelings, and our actions, reactions, or behaviors. It starts off with our thoughts. What we think will influence how we feel. How we feel will affect how we behave or respond. It all starts with our thinking.

Let's say you have a presentation coming up that's in front of your peers or coworkers. You think about all of the bad things that can happen. You think about what will happen if you get nervous. You think about what will happen if you forget your words. You think about what will happen if you feel anxious. Because of those negative thoughts, you feel anxious and stressed about the upcoming presentation. Due to feeling anxious, stressed, and worried, you freak out before the presentation and the negative things you are thinking about, and those feelings become a reality.

However, let's take that same presentation and reframe it in a slightly different way. Let's say you think about how well you prepared for the presentation. You know that all of your coworkers and peers support you and want you to succeed. They are all excited about what you have to say, so you get excited. You think about how everybody will agree with you, and you think about everybody standing up and applauding at the end of your presentation. Because of this positive way of thinking, you feel good and comfortable and confident in your abilities to give the presentation. Because of you feeling that way, you look forward to giving the presentation, and when you do, you do a fantastic job.

The two situations have a different outcome. However, that outcome starts with the way you're thinking. When you change the way you think by changing the pictures you make in your mind, you'll change the way you feel. Because of changing the way you feel, the outcome and your actions and reactions will also be different.

Developing Your Success Mindset

When hypnotically connecting with people, it's crucial that you have an unstoppable mindset. There are four traits you should instill in yourself that can make working with you and connecting with you irresistible.

Studies done with sales professionals have shown that the best sales pros display the four mindset traits below. A salesperson can have outstanding knowledge about their product or service, but someone with the four mindsets below will outsell anyone with superior product knowledge.

The same goes for connecting with people in general. You can know everything about these hypnotic communication styles, however, if you are not confident and comfortable in your abilities to use them, and if you don't use them with purpose, and if you are not passionate, you could fall flat on your face.

Surround Yourself with Good People

One of the best ways to maintain a healthy optimistic mindset is to surround yourself with a community of supportive people. You may have heard "You become those with whom you associate." If you are always associating with negative, drama loving, miserable people, who do you think you'll become? Well, it will be challenging to become anything but that.

When you surround yourself with better people, they will push you to be even better than you are now. That is a good thing. You want to surround yourself with people who challenge you and who help you grow mentally and emotionally.

You might be wondering; how do you surround yourself with better people? Should you cut off the people who are your current friends? Of course not! However, we can set standards and boundaries. Think about people as making deposits and withdrawals to your mental bank account. The people always miserable and sucking the life and energy out of you are making withdrawals from your mental bank account. The people who push you and encourage you to do better things but also who genuinely support you are making deposits to your mental bank account. Be very careful of the ones who are trying to make more withdrawals than deposits. Those are the ones who will also be jealous and resentful if you become more successful than they do. Usually, those friendships dissolve and take care of themselves when you move forward in life, and they don't.

The Four Traits of Successful People

Confident

Did you know that confidence is one of the most attractive traits in a person? Sociologists tell us that people will be more attracted to a confident person who is less attractive physically than they will to a person who is more attractive physically but less confident. Knowing this, if you're not already confident, work more on it. Confidence is the main characteristic that people admire and find attractive. Confidence gives other people a sense of certainty. When you are confident in yourself and your abilities, other people will be more confident in you.

Confidence, when defined by Webster's dictionary, is just a belief in oneself and one's own abilities. Confidence has nothing to do with cockiness, arrogance, narcissism, or anything like that. It is just a belief in your abilities to achieve what you want to accomplish. When I see clients for confidence issues, they usually have a false perception of what confidence is. They may have seen their father being overly confident, and other people viewed him as cocky or arrogant. We find that cockiness and arrogance have nothing to do with confidence, yet those traits and attributes are masks for people's insecurities. People who are arrogant in one part of their lives are usually very doubtful and unsure of themselves another part of their life. Being overly confident, cocky, or arrogant can be a turnoff for many people and can often break rapport.

By now, you know a lot of this book is already about relating to and connecting with other people. Yet when I see people for confidence issues, they are always focused on their own internal feelings. One way to break out of that and become more confident is to focus on how you want the person you are communicating with to feel. Do you want the person you're interacting with to feel low-energy, doubt themselves, and insecure? Or do you want them to feel confident, safe, secure, and comfortable? I hope it's the latter. One way to become more confident in yourself is to take the focus off of your feelings and doubts, and instead think about how you can make the person you're communicating with feel more confident and feel more confident in you. When you feel good about yourself, it's easier for people to feel good about you. And when people feel good about you, it's easier for you to feel good about yourself. People usually want to start with themselves first, however, let's break out of that mentality, and put our focus on how we can make the other person feel more confident about themselves. When we make other people feel more positive, they will feel positive about us too. We can build ourselves up by building up others.

Comfortable

You must be comfortable with using these communication styles, and comfortable with the people with whom you are communicating. Using these communication styles will help people feel more comfortable around you. Therefore, you will feel more comfortable around them. A lot of my clients who report feeling overly nervous or anxious around people are usually concerned with how other people view them. There are three perspectives of self. There is the way we see ourselves, the way other people or the outside world views us, and then there's the way we actually are. These three perspectives rarely line up, which can cause forms of social anxiety or nervousness.

The first step in helping people reduce feelings of nervousness or anxiety is helping them improve their view of themselves. In assisting them to accept themselves and develop their personal view, they can then see themselves in a better light. Then they will have more confidence in how other people view them. That bridges the gap between the way we view ourselves and the way other people view us.

Feeling more comfortable with oneself will help reduce nervousness and anxiety substantially. One great way to feel comfortable with yourself is to get other people to feel comfortable with you. One way that other people will feel comfortable with you is to make them feel good about themselves, and also about communicating with you. That's why it's essential to practice and utilize these techniques because it will help other people feel more comfortable with you. That will give you an advantage over those other people who are too cocky or arrogant to consider other people's comfort.

Purposeful

Do you know someone who talks just to talk? They open their mouth apparently to hear themselves speak? Might they be uncomfortable with awkward silence? And then when they have something important to say, nobody is listening.

When hypnotically communicating with people, you should speak with purpose and intent. Before you open up the lines of communication with people, ask yourself the question, what do I intend in connecting with this person? When you understand your purpose, their purpose, and your intent, you can speak clearly and from a more genuine place.

Being authentic and genuine will help you communicate more with purpose. It also shows you are human and will allow others to connect with you even more. Just know that you are not sharing too much with the wrong group of people. I remember speaking to a large group of business owners, and one person asked me to talk about an obstacle I had to get over and how I got over that obstacle. I described a situation that caused me to have symptoms of PTSD and how I overcame that and moved forward from that. As I was talking about this, people in the room were welling up with tears, and after my presentation, dozens of people were telling me how much my story clicked with them, and how appreciative they were that I shared that story. That one story got me a lot of new clients that day. Many months after this event, I was sitting down with a friend and colleague who was there that day and who heard me speak. He politely criticized me for not maintaining an image of being perfect in front of my customers and clients. He recommended that in future situations, I do not talk about that, and keep that to myself. However, if I did not share about that situation, it would not have helped or affected as many people as it did.

Being honest and genuine requires judgment, and that is where my friend was coming from in criticizing me for revealing an obstacle I went through. Being genuine and authentic is good. However, this comes with balance. You must do this so it builds you up instead of knocking you down. Share enough for the audience that you are giving without sharing too much. For example, do you share your political views and religious views with a group of people you are trying to win over? Probably not unless it's appropriate. However, there is a lot more you can share that will make for a purposeful conversation.

Passionate

Have you ever been in a room with people who are very dull and boring? It sucks the energy right out of you, and it sucks the fun out of the situation, doesn't it? Passion is power, and with it comes energy. Passionate enthusiasm is one trait that can ignite an immediate spark in other people around you, and it is attractive and contagious. When you show energy and passion to other people, they will, in turn, become more energetic.

People who are passionate, get excited and enthusiastic about what they're doing. Can you imagine trying to connect with somebody, but their energy level is so low it seems almost as if they don't care? Imagine going to buy a car from somebody, but to them, it's just another job, and you are just another customer. They couldn't care less if you get what you want, so they will not be excited about working with you, and they will not do their best in meeting all of your needs.

That is also true when going out on a date. Can you imagine going out with somebody, but it seems like the person doesn't want to be there, they're dragging their feet, and it feels almost like they would rather be at home by themselves? We have all had experiences like this. However, when you feel comfortable and confident, when you speak with purpose and intent, and when you're passionate, excited, and enthusiastic, people will want to communicate with you.

Now that you know what it takes to be a master communicator, let's look at some ways to achieve your goals and positively program your mind to get more of what you want in life and to realize your full potential.

Chapter 10

Quick Change Techniques for Building Your Ideal Life

Changing Your Internal Programming

The best way to improve your internal programs by changing your thoughts is through your imagination. Your imagination allows you to try things on your mind before you do them in reality. It's like a rehearsal center that helps to get you ready for the actual event. Throughout this section, you will learn different imagination exercises that will help give you a mental boost, and mindset shift so you can experience more positive thoughts, feelings, and behaviors.

Let's start off with a straightforward strategy that you can start doing right now. I know you've been told before to think positively about everything. However, I'm not convinced that positive thinking will solve all of your problems. There is a way that can help you redirect your thoughts so you feel better.

We are our own best hypnotists. We are already giving ourselves suggestions, but those suggestions are often negative. We are usually so focused on the undesired outcome and what we do not want to do that we get caught up in that negative focus state of mind until it becomes natural. Think of what you're already telling yourself. I bet you've said to yourself several times, "I can't do this." Or even something like, "Why should I even try? Things never work out for me anyway." Too often our internal self-talk is limiting us from doing what we should be able to do.

Imagine you had a friend or someone who lives with you who continually points out everything that you do wrong. They use a harsh tone of voice and point out everything that is wrong with you and everything you do. They are never supportive; they are always so negative about everything you try to do. Would you still be friends with that person? Probably not. If you wouldn't accept this type of negativity and harassment from a friend, why would you allow it from yourself? Believe it or not, this is how many people are talking to themselves every day. Here's one way to break out of that contrary thinking program.

The first thing you must do is to recognize and acknowledge your negative internal dialogue. As soon as it starts, take notice. Once you become aware of it, interrupt it immediately. One way to disrupt that negative thought loop pattern of is to clap your hands and literally shout out the word "STOP" anytime you recognize yourself thinking that way. From there, you want to change the story in your mind. Instead of asking yourself all the bad things that can happen or reminding yourself of how often you failed, think about what it would be like to succeed. Instead of focusing on the consequences of not taking action, focus on the results of taking action. This change in focus may require practice, but eventually, it will become more natural.

By no means am I saying you should be perfect, or even pretend to be perfect. Rather, instead of being your own worst critic, you can be your own greatest cheerleader, cheering yourself on throughout the greatest of victories. And when you are victorious, celebrate it, rejoice, and honestly be happy for yourself. The more you do this, the stronger that pattern will get. You'll be feeling better, and you'll be developing mental toughness and confidence more and more each day.

Changing Your Internal Dialogue

One reason we have negative self-talk as our internal dialogue is often because of what we heard growing up. I can't tell you how often clients have come into my office saying something like, "all I can hear is my mother in my head saying you'll never be good enough," or something along those lines. Here's one way to change the internal sabotaging voice.

Locate the internal voice. Ask yourself where it is. For some people, it's right in the forefront of their mind, for others, it's in the back of their head. Some feel it almost like a weight weighing down on their chest.

The second thing to do is to recognize the tone, the volume, and anything else about the sound. Just ask yourself, how does that voice sound or who does it remind you of? Does it sound like your mother? Does it sound like your father? Does it sound like an ex? Too often, for women who have been abused by an ex-husband, either mentally or physically, report that what they keep hearing in their mind is the ex-husband telling them that they're not good enough.

Now change the voice. All the things you just became aware of, the location, the volume, the tone, etc., change all those things about it. We call this changing submodalities. Push that voice far away as if you're hearing it from across the room now. Lower the volume of the voice. Slow the voice down, or speed it up. I often tell people to hear the voice as if it were coming across the room being said by Mickey Mouse or Elmo. Imagine Mickey Mouse or Elmo saying in a high-pitched squeaky voice from across the room, "You'll never be good enough, you'll never be good enough, you'll never be good enough." It feels much different, doesn't it?

I remember a woman coming into my office so depressed and afraid to do anything new because of an abusive ex-husband. She came in with the identity that she wasn't good enough. She sat down and bawled her eyes out. As she was crying, she wailed out, "All I can hear is my ex-husband saying nobody likes you, you're awful, and I'm going to make sure everybody knows it!"

I didn't want her to suffer any more than she had been, so we used the exercise from above. I asked her to imagine hearing the voice from across the room, but instead of her ex-husband saying those things, to hear it now as a high-pitched voice just like Elmo. I repeated all the things her ex-husband was saying but in a high-pitched squeal like Elmo's voice. The tears immediately stopped, and she cracked up laughing exclaiming, "I never realized how ridiculous that sounds." She had gone to therapy for about three years before coming to see me, and she said, "I've talked about it so much; I learned to break down in tears automatically whenever I think about it. But when you helped me change the voice, I was able to laugh at it for the first time in years and realize how ridiculous those words were when I was hearing them differently." This technique can be powerful.

People might ask, "How is this important in my ability to have a hypnotic connection with people?" Well, if you're continually going to think that people don't like you, or that you're not worthy, or any other negative thoughts, it will be challenging for you to connect with anyone. However, once you learn how to control your internal voice and clear the mental and emotional baggage holding you back; you'll be able to connect with anyone, anywhere, anytime that you want.

Focusing on What You Want

Remember, in the previous section you learned how to get people to do what you want by focusing on desired outcomes instead of what you do *not* want them to do. The same thing applies to you as well. We are programmed to think negatively about things sometimes. It's just a natural defense mechanism to keep us safe and protected to weigh out all outcomes. However, we are completely capable of keeping ourselves safe in situations even without thinking so negatively about them. Many people ask why they're so nervous, or anxious, or stressed even when they know there's no need to be. The reason is that we get more of what has our focus. Usually, people are focused on how they do not want to feel, and as a consequence, they end up feeling that way. It goes back to thoughts, feelings, and actions.

A person will go into a situation and often mentally tell themselves, don't feel nervous, there's no need to be stressed out about this. Logically, they might know that there's no need to feel anxious or nervous. However, the subconscious mind does not understand negative commands or negative words. So, when a person says to themselves, "don't be nervous, don't be anxious, don't be stressed," they're actually giving themselves a hypnotic suggestion to feel nervous, anxious, and stressed.

You might be wondering how we can stop this from happening and rearrange those thoughts in our subconscious mind. We do this by focusing on how we want to feel, think, and behave instead of thinking about how we do not want to think, feel, and behave. When you notice that you're thinking about what you don't want to be, interrupt that thought and frame it around how you want to be or feel. Instead of telling yourself not to feel nervous or anxious, tell yourself, "just relax, feel confident, you know what you're doing, you can do this." It goes back to being your own best cheerleader. The more you start focusing on how you want to feel versus how you don't want to feel, the more you'll begin to re-program that old pattern of behavior in your mind. You'll start to get more of those desired feelings instead of the undesired feelings.

This same technique works as well with how other people are talking to you. I do a lot of work with athletes with very negative coaches. Their coaches are always telling them what not to do instead of telling them what to do. So, the foundation I set for every athlete and also for employees with negative managers and bosses is to rearrange what is said to them. Instead of hearing the negative, they reframe it to the positive. If a boss says to their employee, "don't miss your deadline," the employee should reframe it to, "get your work in on time." Have you ever told somebody not to forget something, and they forget it? Instead of telling them not to forget something, we can suggest what to remember instead of what not to forget. When we talk this way to people, and we start reframing what people tell us, we will feel better, and we will also respond better in situations where we used to doubt ourselves.

Reprogramming Your Powerful Subconscious

One reason people are not more successful is because of the pictures that they're making in their mind. But what if you could rearrange the images you're making, and re-program your mindset so you can experience even more success? This exercise will help you do precisely that. It can help you feel more confident, more comfortable, more passionate and more enthusiastic.

Let's start with a brief exercise. Remember back to a time where you felt terrific and happy. It could be a birthday, a holiday, a time as a child, or even a simple time spent alone, or with other people laughing and enjoying yourself. Just remember back to this time for a moment. As you remember this time, close your eyes. See what you saw, hear what you heard, feel all the good feelings you felt. Go through this memory a couple of times remembering more positive feelings and more great details each and every time. Just stay in that memory for a moment and then open up your eyes.

When you opened your eyes, I bet you felt pretty good. The reason that you're probably feeling good is simple. The subconscious mind cannot tell the difference between a real experience versus a vividly imagined experience. So, when you bring your mind to someplace very calm and comfortable, you feel calm and comfortable. When you bring your mind to a happier place, you feel the feelings associated with that happy place. The same thing is true with the opposite side. When we think about bad times in the past, we will often still feel bad about them even though they're not currently happening. We can re-create any feelings or sensations we want, simply by bringing our mind to times when we felt that way. Watching an image in our mind, or even on a movie screen, will cause us to feel some emotions associated with that. However, if we float into the mental picture we are making, which is what we usually do, will feel those feelings and sensations connected to that picture even more intensely.

Before we dive into the self-hypnosis exercise, you must know a little something about hypnotic receptivity. When a person is in hypnosis, their subconscious mind opens up so they can accept suggestions on a deeper level. One way that hypnotists do this is through utilizing a hypnotic induction process which relaxes the critical mind and allows the subconscious mind to open up. However, these same states happen several times a day naturally. There are two times we know for sure this happens that can be controlled by you. Our subconscious mind is more active and open when falling asleep at night and as we are waking up in the morning. That's why some people will wake up in the morning to an alarm clock radio, and the first song that they heard when they awoke will rattle around in their head all day long, and they don't know how or why it stuck in their mind. The same thing is happening when people will sometimes dream about a television program they were watching as they fall asleep.

How can we apply these two principles to overall self-improvement?

The first thing to do is pick out a goal you have in mind. It might be a behavior you want to change, or a way you want to feel, or any other goal you have. It could be to be more confident and more comfortable when you're connecting with people or to improve a relationship with these communication strategies, or some other goal.

As you're falling asleep, imagine you are in a movie theater, and there's a big screen in front of you. On the movie screen, make a big picture of yourself feeling how you want to feel in whatever situation you're imagining. See yourself already having achieved the goal you are thinking about in your mind. Make this movie in your mind big and clear. Use your imagination with this one. Remember, the subconscious mind cannot tell the difference between a real experience and a vividly imagined experience. Create this image in as much detail as possible. Once you create this image, turn up the sounds, the colors, the intensity and even the brightness and definition of this picture. Play it over a couple of times in your mind — noticing new things each and every time you play it over in your mind. Now, jump back to the beginning, and float into the movie so you can see things through your eyes, hear things through your ears, and feel and sense things through your mind and body. See yourself as if you were actually that person now. Experience the feelings, sights, and sounds associated with this picture. Once you experience them, float these things back into you.

By doing this exercise, you are activating your imagination, and signaling your subconscious mind. Your subconscious mind will help awaken all the attributes, traits, characteristics, and belief systems associated with this picture to make it more likely for you to achieve the goal you have in mind.

For maximum effectiveness, repeat the same exercise as you're waking up in the morning. This routine will start your day off on a good note, and help you feel positive throughout the day as you associate mentally with your ability to achieve your goal.

Feeling Calm, Relaxed and Balanced in Any Situation

During the time I have been a Board-Certified Hypnotist, I have worked with nearly every problem you could imagine. I've worked with clients regarding weight issues, smoking issues, sexual difficulties, traumas, murder investigations, sports performance, sales performance, anxiety, stress, fears, phobias, and many more areas. After working with tens of thousands of people on these various issues, I saw one common theme that consistently held people back from achieving their end goal. That one obstacle is stress.

Stress can take on many forms. For some people, a particular person such as a spouse, an ex, a boss or co-worker, or situation, or even a memory or thought can cause feelings of stress and anxiety. When people feel stressed, anxious, nervous, or any other manifestation of stress, it usually means they are not performing as well as they could be. I also find that stress holds people back from making well-informed decisions. When you go into a situation stressed-out and anxious, you're usually not thinking clearly, your mind is clouded and cluttered, and often you say or do things you may regret.

Stress can also be the main problem that causes people to indulge or partake in bad habits and even addictions. How many people do you know who eat when they feel stressed? How many people do you know who smoke when they feel stressed? How many people do you know who shop too much when they're stressed? How many people do you know who feel so stressed it makes them sick? I'm sure you can put at least one or two people in each category. You may even fall into one of these categories as well.

Stress does not just cause us to act irrationally or cause us to give in to bad habits. It can also cause many health complications as well such as heart disease, high blood pressure, and even death. Yes, unfortunately, there are thousands of people reported each year who die because of stress-related illnesses.

Stress not only affects your mind and your well-being, but it also affects everybody else around you. Imagine arriving at work or school one day, and one of your coworkers or peers has been in an argument with their boyfriend or girlfriend. They talk to you about it, and then they get other people involved asking their advice as well. Now their stress and their problems have become your stress and your problems.

You might argue that it's not your problem, and as the saying goes, not my monkeys and not my circus, but if you try to counsel them or give them advice, it becomes your problem. It affects your job and your ability to perform at the level you should. It becomes distracting to everybody around you as well who has to listen to all those problems and negativity.

This book wouldn't be complete if we did not address ways that can help manage your stress. You're going to learn straightforward exercises that you can do to help deal with your feelings of stress, anxiety, nervousness, worry, and tension.

Many issues that keep us from achieving our goals trace back to the stress we carry in our lives. Often, these issues such as pain, negative thoughts, habits (like smoking or nail-biting), overeating, etc. all stem from stress. In my hypnosis practice, my clients are eager to learn powerful self-hypnosis exercises that help them overcome their obstacles. In the remainder of the book, you will learn a selection of the most powerful and effective self-hypnotic techniques that can help you make improvements in your own life.

Self-Hypnosis Exercises to Build Your Ideal Life

In 2015, I had the pleasure and opportunity to give a TEDx talk which went viral on YouTube. It was all about how self-hypnosis can help you live a better life. I attribute a lot of the successes I have had and my keen ability to overcome obstacles to my being diligent in using self-hypnosis exercises to re-program my thought process about things. The techniques I use are exactly how I work with my clients.

After seeing thousands of clients, I have picked out some of the most useful and powerful exercises I used to help them, and I have included them in this book so they can help you as well.

To get you started seeing results and experiencing more success, I have focused here on three topics that help transform people's lives.

These three areas are:

Stress and anxiety

Confidence and a high-performing mental attitude

Motivation and taking consistent action

Stress and Anxiety

Stress and anxiety can manifest itself in many forms. It can take manifest as worry, fear, doubt, low self-esteem, negative thinking, to name a few. This stress and anxiety can be a huge obstacle that hinders people from living their ideal lives. Stress and anxiety can prevent people from taking action, it can prevent people from feeling confident, and it can get in the way of achieving our goals or improving personal and professional relationships. Once you learn how to control stress and anxiety, you can build a bigger and better life where you conquer fear instead of it letting it control you!

Confidence

As I mentioned, confidence is a feeling and a belief in oneself and one's abilities. However, lack of confidence and self-doubt issues usually stem from anxiety. Once you learn how to control stress and anxiety, you can build a more confident state of mind. Confidence and reducing anxiety go hand in hand. Reducing anxiety is a part of boosting confidence and eliminating self-doubt is a surefire way to build more confidence and self-accepting attitude.

Motivation and Consistent Action

Stress and anxiety, as well as lack of confidence, hold us back from taking action and being productive. These can lead to putting things off and procrastinating on the things we should do. Building motivation and eliminating procrastination can help us take action and become more successful professionally, personally and even with our relationships with others. Say goodbye to constantly putting things off and embrace the action-taking abilities you will see as more of a consistent theme in your life.

Using Other Influences to Make These Exercises More Powerful

When doing the exercises listed below, you can add other layers that can make them more successful. These can be sounds such as music or even scents such as lighting a candle. For the relaxation exercise, you can try playing calming music, for the motivation exercise, you can try playing fast, energetic music, and for confidence, think of something like the theme from the movie *Rocky*.

You can also change things about your situation. One of my close friends has motivational quotes lining the walls of her office because she wants people to feel motivated every time they walk into her office. In her reception area, there is soft lighting, and relaxing music and candles lit because she wants that to feel more relaxed and welcoming.

When doing these exercises, think about what you can change or add to your situation or setting to make the activities more effective. As I write this part of the book right now, I have my Pandora playing "The Piano Guys" station to keep me focused; I have a motivational poster in the background with a quote on it, there is a salt lamp to my right and a peppermint candle to my left. I made the atmosphere conducive to how I want to be. Just by making small adjustments to your atmosphere, you will find yourself feeling the way you choose.

The Movies in Our Minds

Remember when I asked you to put yourself into a positive memory, and you felt good just by bringing your mind to that memory? In this section, we will create a positive association or link positive feelings with a minimal action or trigger. This trigger will anchor these feelings of calmness and relaxation into you, so whenever you activate the trigger, it will cause a flow of positive emotions and thoughts to go through your mind and body.

Your subconscious mind does not know the difference between that which is vividly imagined or actually happening. That's why when we go to a movie theater and watch a movie, we experience the emotions portrayed in the film. When you see a scary movie, you jump when the directors want you to jump. When you see a happy or funny movie, you laugh and feel good when the directors want you to laugh and feel good. And when you watch a sad movie, you cry at the sad parts. In fact, if you're anything like me, you've seen the movie *The Notebook* nineteen times and still cry every single time at the end (SPOILER ALERT) when the two older adults die at the end of the film.

The question is why do we still feel these emotions and experience these sensations even though consciously and analytically we know actors are playing a role, reciting a script in a scene with lights and cameras? Movies and experiences like this engage the imagination. Emotions, feelings, and sensations are functions of the subconscious mind and not the conscious mind. Therefore, when we watch a movie, our subconscious mind doesn't know if it's currently happening in front of us or if it's just a story that's being played out on a movie screen. So, we feel the emotions as if it was a reality, happening in front of us. The same principle applies to the exercise you will learn now.

The Calm Trigger

I often get referrals from doctors and from the court system of people who have so much stress and anxiety it causes rage and anger issues, and in turn, causes people to act irrationally. These people have usually been through years of therapy and considered as "non-responsive to traditional therapeutic intervention."

One woman had so much anger and stress built up that she was becoming a danger to herself and others. Using this technique and others similar, I taught her how to take control of her stress responses quickly and how to increase her feelings of being calm, relaxed and in control. I worked with her to practice the technique, which allowed her to relax and feel calm quickly until it became a natural way of responding. Many of my clients call it "The Calm Trigger" or "The Calm Button." Once they implement it, they can access a state of relaxation within just a few seconds so the things that would have bothered them now cause them to feel more balanced, more in control, and calmer.

This calm trigger works as a boat anchor helps the boat stay steady and still even in the rough waters. An emotional connection (anchor) helps you to be calm and access a state of self-control even when things get rocky throughout your daily life. One difference between a boat anchor and an emotional trigger is that your emotional trigger gets stronger and better the more you use it.

Many of the psychology intellectuals will also see the similarity between this and classical conditioning (which is a form of hypnosis). Do you remember learning about the study of Pavlov's dogs in psychology 101?

The Russian psychologist Ivan Pavlov conditioned his German shepherd dogs to salivate every time he rang a bell. He conditioned them by ringing a bell every time he presented them with food. Soon, the dogs formed a link, association or "anchor/trigger" between the ringing of the bell and the food. Once that association between the bell and the food was "anchored" into their nervous system, he just rang a bell, and the dogs would respond the same way as they would if they were about to be fed. The same thing happens when you reach for your dog's leash, and they jump with excitement that they get to go for a walk.

The exercise you are about to learn uses the same conditioning and will help you create an inner feeling of being calm, relaxed and in control as a regular and natural part of your day so that things that used to bother you about your day will now have a calming effect. You can also use this technique to spread the feeling of relaxation into more areas of your life. Soon, you will be responding in a more balanced and calm state of mind.

The Calm Trigger Exercise

Before you practice this technique, read through the steps first so you know what to do.

Recall and remember a time when you felt very calm and relaxed. You felt calm, relaxed and in control. It could be a vacation spot, a time lying in bed, or just a time where you felt good. In your mind, go back to that place now and see what you saw, hear what you heard and feel the feelings you felt. Some people will find they cannot remember a relaxing time, often because they are already caught up in a stress response and cannot come up with the "perfect time" when they felt good. If this is the case for you, let yourself imagine how good it would feel to be completely relaxed and to have all the balance, comfort, and self-control you could ever want and need. Think about what happens when you feel relaxed and in control.

Run this experience through your mind and make everything bigger, brighter, and better. Make the sounds and sights more intense and put it in high definition. Make the positive feelings as strong as you can. Turn them up as if you had a dial next to you that controls these feelings from this time.

When feeling these good feelings and thoughts, press your right thumb and index finger together (like you were making an "OK" sign) and rub those two fingers together. By doing this, you are creating an association between this feeling and this touch. You form a link between this physical action and the positive emotion behind it. Run through this positive thought or memory several times until you feel that feeling of inner calm, relaxed and in control.

Go through this memory at least five more times while rubbing your right thumb and index finger together. Allow this action to connect with these pleasant thoughts and feelings, so every time and any time you need to feel this good feeling, you just rub those fingers together, and it brings your mind back to how good you can feel.

You will know that you have created the "trigger" when you rub those fingers together and you can easily remember the feelings of being calm, relaxed and in control as they spread through your mind and body.

Now let's put this to the test. Think about a situation you would have found mildly stressful in the past. Once again, rub those two fingers together. Feel the feelings of calmness, relaxation and in control running through your mind and body and imagine or think about taking this calm feeling into that stressful situation. Imagine yourself approaching this situation with more balance and calmness and imagine how things are now different. Imagine everything going as well as it could be. See what you want to see. Hear what you want to hear. Feel the good feelings and sensations that you get from this now. It feels much easier to control the situation now.

Still rubbing your fingers together, remember the calm feelings of being balanced and in control. Again, imagine being in that situation you used to perceive as stressful. This time, imagine a few challenges popping up, but notice yourself handling those challenges perfectly. See, hear, and feel everything that you need to about how you are calm and in control.

Finally, stop and think about that situation now. Notice the difference in how you are thinking about it and feeling about it now, versus just a few minutes ago. Repeat the exercise several times as necessary until you notice a shift.

Each time you do this exercise, it will become easier and better as it becomes more conditioned into your subconscious mind.

You can do this any time you need to feel more calm, relaxed, and safe. You can do this any time anywhere, and nobody will even know you are doing anything.

An additional layer you can add to this exercise is to give this good relaxing feeling a color, and as you rub the fingers together, just imagine that good feeling takes on the calming and soothing color and circulate that color through your body and mind. As it kicks out the bad, it replaces the negative feelings with the good, powerful, and positive feelings.

Boost Your Confidence Exercise

The next is a technique I do with a lot of athletes and sales professionals to increase their mental state, establish instant confidence, and develop an attitude of high performance. This exercise will put you into a better mental and physical state. It starts with identifying a situation where you could use more confidence.

Think of a person who you view as more confident than yourself. Imagine a person who can handle the situations that you may experience. They could tackle anything head-on with confidence and high levels of self-esteem.

Imagine that they are standing in front of you about to enter into the situation where you've doubted yourself. See in your imagination how they are standing, notice what their body language is and how they conduct themselves.

Now see them going through the situation and notice how they'd be talking, interacting, or performing.

Jump back to the beginning of the scene and float into this person right before they are about to go into the situation. Notice what they would be thinking, notice how they would be feeling, and listen to what they would be telling themselves. Make those adjustments within yourself by imagining that you have the traits and qualities of this person.

Imagine going through this situation as if you were this person.

Rewind the situation, back to the beginning, and now walk through it again as you, but this time doing everything the same way your "ideal person" would do it. See what you'd see, hear what you'd hear, and feel and think what you'd need to for it to go perfectly, with confidence and a high performing mental attitude.

Repeat this exercise several times.

I also like to call this exercise "Stealing Confidence." You are basically reprograming your response by modeling behavior of someone whom you view as more confident and able to go through a particular situation with confidence and ease. This person can be a person you know, a celebrity, or even someone you have created in your imagination.

Motivation Button

These hypnotic techniques are all about forming cognitive associations with memories that create a flow of positive feelings and emotions that drive you to succeed. In this exercise, we will create a link between a memory when you felt you were taking consistent action towards a goal and an action of making a fist with your dominant hand. Follow the steps below, and read through each step before you do the exercise.

Rate how strong your motivation is on a scale of 1–10 regarding doing something you need to do to achieve a goal. One is the weakest and ten is the strongest.

Think of something that you are already motivated to do. Make this something about which you feel strongly or passionately. It can be a favorite hobby or activity you like, being with a friend or loved one, or even going to a special place you really enjoy. If you can't think of something, ask yourself how motivated you'd be to collect your winnings if you won the lottery, or even think of how motivated you'd be to take a shower after you just rolled around in mud, dirt, and filth. I bet that motivation would be pretty high. Or think about if you went on a camping trip and you forgot your toothbrush, and you couldn't brush your teeth for a week. You had a film building up on your teeth. Imagine how motivated you'd be to get home and brush those teeth!

Whatever motivates you the most at this time, visualize the scene. See what you'd see, hear what you'd hear, and feel and sense what you'd feel. Feel exactly what it's like to be motivated — notice all the details about this scene. Make everything bigger, brighter, and more intense. As the feelings heighten and peak, make a fist with your dominant hand. As you squeeze that fist, make everything stronger.

Keep going through this motivational scene as if it were a movie. As soon as it ends, loop it back to the beginning again. Feeling the motivation even stronger this time all the while squeezing your hand into a fist.

Now give this feeling a location in your body, give the motivating feeling a color, and let this feeling and color spread through your entire body as you squeeze that fist.

Stop, and relax.

Now that you have done that, let's test your motivation trigger. Once again, squeeze that fist and re-experience that good feeling again now. You may not feel it as intense, and if you don't just replay that motivational movie again in your mind as you squeeze that fist. Notice where that motivation starts in your body. Give it a color and spread the feeling throughout your entire body.

Let's create the link now. Make the fist again and remember that motivation. Now imagine yourself taking action and feeling amazing about getting this thing done that you have been putting off! See yourself completing this task or following through on what you need to confidently and see yourself feeling amazing about this! As soon as you have done that, go through this again. Each time you make that fist, permanently associate that motivation and taking action with clenching your fist.

Let's rate your motivation towards completing your goal right now. On a scale of 1–10, how motivated do you feel about your goal now? The higher the number, the easier you will find it to take action. If the number is still small, practice the exercise until you notice spikes in your motivation.

Chapter 11

Bringing Everything Full Circle

Connecting with Yourself to Better Connect with Others

Part of connecting with others is to boost up your mental attitude. Now that you know several ways to change and control your feelings and emotions, you can now approach things with a better mental attitude and better connect with others.

Success happens because of your ability to take action and also in having a winning and magnetic personality. When you are more successful, people will enjoy being around you much more, and they will want to emulate you.

Even the people who you think have everything and are living perfect lives still work on themselves and see self-improvement and success as a journey and a movement they make happen consistently in their lives. They are always asking themselves questions that continue to motivate them and see solutions to do better in their lives. These are questions we call "power questions."

Here are five powerful questions you can use that will lead towards creating more consistent action and success in your life:

What is stopping me from having what I want?

What must I do or stop doing to have what I want?

What will it be like once I have what I want?

What resources do I need to get closer to what I want?

What is the first smallest step I can take to move closer to what I want?

People who are successful and seem to have everything they could ever want in life also recognize the pain and pleasure principle. People want to move away from pain — pain gets them to take action. Purpose and pleasure keep that action going and consistent so they can run across the finish line and achieve their goals.

The Perfect Balance

Too much of a good thing is never a good thing. Remember when we were talking about how being overly confident can come off as being arrogant or cocky? The same thing is true with the traits above. You don't want to be too overly excited, or you may seem phony. You don't want to be overly confident, or you'll seem too arrogant. You don't want to be too relaxed, because then you will lack energy. At the same token, if you're overthinking about every single word that's coming out of your mouth, you'll sound like a robot.

There has to be a balance of the mindsets we listed above of confidence, comfort, passionate enthusiasm, and purpose. When you have the perfect balance of these mindsets, you'll be able to create a hypnotic connection with anyone. You will have a good view of yourself, other people will feel good about being around you, and people will get to see the real side of who you are. The gap between the three perspectives of self will be less, and you'll feel good about other people wanting to do things for you.

Will You Fall for This Now?

I always love it when people who attend my presentations say, "I'd never fall for that stuff, I'm too smart for that!" Well, it has nothing to do with being too smart or too gullible. In fact, you're not falling for anything! All that I've described is natural human behavior. It's all in the way we communicate, but now you will be aware of these communication styles, and you can communicate with purpose!

Communicating with Purpose and Intent

The more meaning behind your communication with people, the better results you will notice. As you think about how you want other people to feel, act, behave, and respond to you, your products, and your services, the better the outcomes will be. An excellent way to practice these techniques is to pick one or two per week and become open to and aware of opportunities where you can use them until they feel comfortable and become natural. Soon you will notice a drastic improvement in the power of your words when there is meaning and thought behind them.

Take Action

The people who get the best results are those who take consistent action. Some techniques in this book will get the most immediate results, whereas others may require repetition and time to develop as any good skill does. Let these tools and skills provide you with a competitive advantage over other people. Some of the best communicators in the world use these skills and aren't aware of them, whereas others who are also great communicators are acutely aware of how and what they are communicating and to whom.

The tools that you learned in this book will provide you with the skills to influence those around you. These skills, when used consistently, will also help you re-program your thoughts, your feelings, and your behaviors so you can live an even better life.

I hope you've found this book enlightening, helpful, and most importantly, motivating to look at how you meet and interact with people right now and what you can do to improve in that area. Best of luck and keep working on those skills and methods. Start by picking one or two little things you can try and implement them.

Then come back to this book again and again until you become the person you want to be. That person, who works well with others, wins others over to your side and keeps making progress in life until it's the way you've always envisioned it. Life's a journey, and we should work every day on becoming better at it.

So, go out there, take action, influence people, and have fun while doing it.

Success is a journey; it's not a final destination. To help people take consistent action along their paths, I have created a private group called "The Make Success Happen Inner Circle." The members get monthly coaching, strategies, and mental conditioning exercises to make sure that they stay on the road to success in all areas of their lives. If you'd like to continue what you've learned here and join my inner circle, head over to www.dancandell.com.

As I tell my clients — Always remember, be well, do good, and be true to who you are.